# Communicating Aggression in a Megamedia World

This book describes how, in the era of megamedia culture, aggression in communication constitutes a threat to the communication community.

Based on the theoretical incorporation of transcendental pragmatics, the book explores how conceptualizing the phenomena of megamedia aggression from this perspective and diagnosing their destructive force are essential for: postulating the need for constructing a theory of media communication closely related to the model of discursive rationality, giving this theory a critical and normative character, and embedding it in the perspective of the project of social co-responsibility and in the plan for an ethics of co-responsibility.

Combining key elements of media theory, the philosophy of communication, the concept of normative ethics, and the fields of social psychology and social anthropology, this book will be of great interest to scholars and students in the areas of communication studies, philosophy, anthropology, psychology, and psychoanalysis.

**Beata Sierocka** is a professor at the University of Lower Silesia. The two main fields of her research are communication philosophy and philosophical criticism. Her most important publications include *Prolegomena to Philosophical Criticism, Criticism and Discourse*, and the series of articles entitled *Via communicandi*, which develop the theory of communicative rationality.

# Routledge Focus on Communication Studies

**A Relational Model of Public Discourse**
The African Philosophy of Ubuntu
*Leyla Tavernaro-Haidarian*

**Communicating Science and Technology through Online Video**
Researching a New Media Phenomenon
*Edited by Bienvenido León and Michael Bourk*

**Strategic Communication and Deformative Transparency**
Persuasion in Politics, Propaganda, and Public Health
*Isaac Nahon-Serfaty*

**Globalism and Gendering Cancer**
Tracking the Trope of Oncogenic Women from the US to Kenya
*Miriam O'Kane Mara*

**Maatian Ethics in a Communication Context**
*Melba Vélez Ortiz*

**Enhancing Intercultural Communication in Organizations**
Insights from Project Advisers
*Edited by Roos Beerkens, Emmanuelle Le Pichon,
Roselinde Supheert, Jan D. ten Thije*

**Communicating Aggression in a Megamedia World**
*Beata Sierocka*

# Communicating Aggression in a Megamedia World

**Beata Sierocka**

NEW YORK AND LONDON

First published 2021
by Routledge
605 Third Avenue, New York, NY 10158

and by Routledge
2 Park Square, Milton Park, Abingdon, Oxon, OX14 4RN

*Routledge is an imprint of the Taylor & Francis Group, an informa business*

© 2021 Beata Sierocka

The right of Beata Sierocka to be identified as authors of this work has been asserted by her in accordance with sections 77 and 78 of the Copyright, Designs and Patents Act 1988.

Translation © 2021 Elżbieta Frąckowiak

All rights reserved. No part of this book may be reprinted or reproduced or utilised in any form or by any electronic, mechanical, or other means, now known or hereafter invented, including photocopying and recording, or in any information storage or retrieval system, without permission in writing from the publishers.

*Trademark notice*: Product or corporate names may be trademarks or registered trademarks, and are used only for identification and explanation without intent to infringe.

*Library of Congress Cataloging-in-Publication Data*
Names: Sierocka, Beata, author.
Title: Communicating aggression in a megamedia world / Beata Sierocka.
Description: New York, NY : Routledge, 2021. | Series: Routledge focus in communication studies | Includes bibliographical references and index.
Identifiers: LCCN 2020055444 (print) | LCCN 2020055445 (ebook) | ISBN 9780367649012 (hardback) | ISBN 9781003126867 (ebook)
Subjects: LCSH: Communication—Philosophy. | Communication—Social aspects. | Aggressiveness. | Violence in mass media.
Classification: LCC P91 .S4626 2021 (print) | LCC P91 (ebook) | DDC 303.601/4—dc23
LC record available at https://lccn.loc.gov/2020055444
LC ebook record available at https://lccn.loc.gov/2020055445

ISBN: 978-0-367-64901-2 (hbk)
ISBN: 978-0-367-64903-6 (pbk)
ISBN: 978-1-003-12686-7 (ebk)

Typeset in Times New Roman
by codeMantra

# Contents

Intro: Mutilated Communication Community  1

**PART I**
**The World**  3

1  Aggression  5
2  The World in the Chains of Megamedia  18
3  Aggression in the Megamedia World  28

**PART II**
**Communication Philosophy**  39

4  Communicative *A Priori*  41
5  Mutualism, Co-Intentionality, Trust  55
6  Rigor of Discursive Rationality  68

**PART III**
**Ethics of Media Communication**  77

7  Public Responsibility of the Media  79
8  Co-responsibility  89

| 9 | Toward a Normative Media Theory | 99 |
| --- | --- | --- |
|   | Conclusion: To Protect οἶκος | 113 |

*References* 115
*Index* 125

# Intro
## Mutilated Communication Community

"Human institutions should emerge, as such, from reasonable conversation." This brief phrase worded by Karl-Otto Apel is one of the most beautiful and accurate sententiae arising from contemporary philosophy.

Nonetheless, it is also a thought in which everything demands deep and detailed reflection and which, even more importantly, raises serious concerns. Specifically, it brings to light concerns about the very possibility of such a conversation, the conditions under which it can take place, and the threats to which it is exposed. Naturally, such a thought also demands an explanation of what "rationality" of our conversation entails—not only that of today, yesterday, or of that from centuries and millennia ago, but ultimately the one which as the "(transcendental) meta-institution of all other human institutions" (Apel 1976, p. 102), universally present in our communication cooperation, invariably conditioning and shaping this cooperation.

Today, our conversation takes place under specific conditions, including new media reality, which strongly transforms all dimensions of reality, both on the level of social and political phenomena and on that of psychological and spiritual ones. This raises new questions and concerns, which are guided by long-time curiosity and anxiety as to how to shape this "reason"; how to protect rationality and maintain its stability; and, above all, how to prevent its destruction, which in the history of mankind—especially in its recent history—has already affected rationality strongly and dramatically.

This anxiety is definitely gaining strength in the face of many negative and very acute phenomena that are created by today's media space—the space which, in view of its specific shape, is legitimately perceived and described as "megamedia." Within it, the magnitude of communicative aggression, whether overt or direct and indirect (and in some way concealed), is particularly disturbing. In every form, it is equally devastating.

Nonetheless, the actual recognition of its destructive power, the understanding of its scope, and ultimately the essence of aggression observed in today's media space are issues that we are just facing and require a well-established theoretical background, primarily in the field of communication research. This is an urgent task given that, both in philosophy and in the empirical disciplines, this issue has been largely neglected—even ignored and forgotten—throughout its long history. For several decades, philosophy and other sciences (including completely new disciplines and fields of research) have been compensating for this negligence. We owe these efforts a completely new viewpoint at the everlastingly penetrated areas of the human world. We owe them, first of all, the indication of communication cooperation as the sphere that shapes social reality, constitutes the essence of man as *homo communicativus*, and builds the communication community with the layers of meanings and sense that determine it. These contents are primarily the work of perspicacity of such theoreticians as Karl-Otto Apel, Jürgen Habermas, Hans-Georg Gadamer, or Michael Tomasello. All these findings—although it would be more legitimate to say "discoveries"—ultimately (in a more or less direct form) led to the emergence of a completely new philosophical subdiscipline: constitution of communication philosophy. It is the role of communication philosophy to conceptualize the communication space to facilitate capturing of specificity of today's media communication; to diagnose the phenomena of aggression observed within it; and, finally, to reveal the mechanisms that determine the condition of the communication community and rationality that organizes it.

These are tasks of exceptional difficulty but also of absolutely exceptional importance because the game is at stake here: to maintain the conditions for existence of the communication community in order to protect it from "fatal" mutilations. Although it is not easy to see, this is the threat posed by aggression that has overcome the media space today.

# Part I
# The World

# 1 Aggression

Aggressive or gentle? Hostile or friendly? Cruel or compassionate? What is the real face of the human? What belongs to human nature? Although struggles with these questions have consumed much time and effort, we still return to them, and we still cannot decide: are humans good or evil in their very essence? The question of evil has always accompanied philosophy. Scientifically formulated questions about aggression, violence, cruelty, and hostility appeared about a century ago and have persisted, with an endless numbers of resolutions.

Most importantly, there have been various attempts to define and specify aggression and violence—and in these contexts also constraint, oppression, and cruelty. Each of these attempts contains a suggestion about the source and potential of these phenomena, and offers a glimmer of hope that they might be mitigated and even overcome. There have also been efforts of diverse provenance to conceptualize and classify the phenomena of aggression; determine their geneses; explain their mechanisms; and identify their types, goals, and perspectives. Consequently, various attempts to diagnose the sources of evil have been made since the beginnings of European philosophy, defining the specific framework of contemporary conceptualizations of aggression. These attempts have usually been theodicy projects—projects, in fact, seeking ways to justify evil. The map of decisions generated by all these attempts is extremely varied. And the number of attitudes toward aggression developed is difficult to count.

From where does this multitude stem? From where does this diversity of competitive resolutions and many reciprocally irreconcilable attitudes result? Is it an effect of our cognitive impotence? Is it a weakness of intellectual tools? Or is it still a question of methodological shortcomings? Presumably, each of these circumstances plays a role, to a certain extent; however, they are not decisive.

The very **nature** of aggression, constituted of a very **complicated network** of conditions, a **multitude** of forms, and an almost limitless **spectrum of consequences**, seems to be decisive and, in fact, conditions this variety of opinions. It is the very complex nature of aggression (as well as violence, hostility, and cruelty) that seems to set the wide scope of historically recorded solutions and concepts explaining it.

Semantic complexities related to the category of aggression or violence undoubtedly are also crucial to the multiplication of theoretical solutions. Moreover, to a certain degree, the whole theoretical situation has been complicated by the difficulties arising from the traditional dispute over universals (which is still not outdated—it is simply a dispute over general concepts). These last two circumstances offer a valuable, fundamental caution when applying the concepts involved to the study of aggression. They warn us against hypostases and sensitize us to all those traps to which the categorical structure of every intellectual (not only philosophical) construction is exposed. Wittgenstein's inquiries or Adorno's negative dialectic—the philosophical concepts so different in their form and yet so unanimous in intention—also subtly sensitize us to those traps. Although these issues are extremely interesting and equally important, it is necessary to disregard them here.

We must realize that the **multiplicity and diversity of concepts** that diagnose the phenomena of aggression (violence and hostility) reflect their complex nature. Most importantly, we must recognize that this diversity should be seen not only as a source of theoretical complications but also as a chance for a comprehensive diagnosis of aggression and, thus, more effective therapy against it.

To capture the map of these concepts and their distribution and distinctive features with one "theoretical look," it must be understood that the main tension and the most important axis of theoretical disputes concerning the phenomena of aggression (as well as violence, hostility, and cruelty) are determined by the answer to the question of **whether aggression belongs to human nature**. This question seems to be concise and clear, but as we will see, this question is neither concise nor clear. Its very formulation hides very strong and problematic assumptions, which have serious consequences. Consequently, one might doubt whether the question is properly formulated at all.

Nevertheless, the answers it has produced determine the most important theoretical distinctions and strongest differentiations among the individual concepts of aggression (regardless of whether they formulate the question *expressis verbis*). And most importantly, these answers decide how the possibilities of controlling and even regulating aggression are perceived.

What does the map of the decisions they outline look like?

The crucial factor, which is obvious in the case of decisive questions, is that the answer to the question of whether aggression pertains to human nature may be short: *yes* or *no*. And these short answers construct the whole map.

The traumatic experiences of the first half of the 20th century—the cruelty of both world wars, the criminal ideologies of 20th-century totalitarianism, and even the brutality of expansive commercialization—prompted the conviction that aggression is a natural feature of human. Historical arrangements, social conditions, and personal experiences are, at most, factors that trigger our instinct or drive for aggression; these are the factors activating the appropriate energy, genotype, or neuron structure. The answer is an unequivocal "Yes"—human aggressiveness is driven by nature.

Powerful scientific authorities stood on the side of this resolution, researchers with highly significant achievements advocated for it, and creators of groundbreaking theoretical paradigms defended it. Yet none of them managed to bear the burden of this problem. None determined its complexity. And most importantly, none presented tools that could effectively control aggression.

Sigmund Freud failed to render it in his psychological concept, according to which aggression, as an innate urge derived from the damaging instinct of self-destruction, takes the form of destructive force accumulating in us and seeking a cathartic outlet (Freud 1922).

Konrad Lorenz failed to determine it in his biological and ethological theory pointing to aggressive energy as a natural drive (inseparable from our nature and evolutionarily formed) ensuring, like the other three main drives, individual reproductive success and thus maintaining the species (Lorenz 1966).

Sociobiologists, led by Edward Wilson, failed with their evolutionary concept, according to which aggressive reactions, just like altruistic reactions, are the indispensable instruments of natural selection embedded in the deep structures of human nature, shaped both evolutionarily and culturally, genetically fixed and natural in both animal and *Homo sapiens* behavior (Wilson 1978).

Finally, contemporary behavioral genetics, which investigates the heritability of human behavior and thus, by searching for a possible "genotype of aggression," points to its genetic conditioning, copes with the comprehensive approach to the problem of aggression to an equally unsatisfactory degree (Plomin 2008).

The fact that none of these concepts (and only those with the widest scope are named here) has guaranteed unquestionable resolutions to the problem of aggression does not mean that none of them have indisputable theoretical value. Each one has been a powerful, influential, inspiring project, revealing its potential and providing unexpected theoretical impulses. Principally, each one, at its deepest level supporting the conviction that aggression pertains to human nature, has the value that it does not allow understating the determinants of aggression independent of our will and does not permit theoretical nonchalance toward them. Each of these concepts, though to a different extent and to a different range, forces humility toward the feature given to us by nature and, at the same time, obliges action to somehow allow wise "distribution" of the aggressive energy to take control over it and even suppress it.

The second part of the map reconstructed here is covered by the concepts that, unlike the previous ones, do not accept the view that aggression pertains to human nature. Frequently, these theories arose from resistance to the aforementioned resolutions. This resistance often emerged not so much from theoretical reasons but from a deep fear that the perception of aggression as woven into human nature is synonymous with its justification and helps people get rid of their responsibility for it. Therefore, as formulated by Erich Fromm in relation to Lorenz's concept, the main role in the emergence of this resistance was played by the fear that the theory of innate aggressiveness easily turns into an ideology that soothes fear and rationalizes the feeling of powerlessness (Fromm 1973). Arguably, this fear (not only in Fromm's work) stemmed from the same reasons that lay behind the conviction of violent human nature: the dread caused by 20th-century genocidal traumas.[1]

Concepts that sensitize us to situational, social, existential, and spiritual conditioning of aggression have been located in this second part of our map. These theories find their origins in this area. The impacts of this area explain both the formation of aggressive behavior and its unique power of destruction.

Many authorities have supported these concepts. Much valuable research was devoted to them and revealed many unexpected connections and dependencies. However, none of the theoreticians in this group managed to create a comprehensive approach to the problem of aggression. And none of the concepts equipped us with a satisfying set of tools through which we could hope to recognize, counteract, regulate, and even eliminate the phenomena of aggression from the human world.

One of the first widely known and highly influential concepts in this group was the theory of frustration-aggression proposed in the 1930s by researchers from Yale University (Dollard 1939).[2] Even though their fundamental thesis that every frustration breeds aggression and that every aggression has its source in some kind of frustration was quite strongly rejected, it provoked interesting theoretical modifications (Berkowitz 1973) and significantly mobilized the social sciences' debate on aggression. The very idea of frustration as a source of aggression, beyond the sphere of influence of the Yale concept, gave impetus to very valuable, multi-threaded research (carried out, for example, based on the existential analysis of Viktor Frankl (1985) and as part of the concept of pain threshold by Joachim Bauer (2011)). The value of this research was revealed primarily in the subtle nuance of this approach it allowed, especially for an understanding of the sources and types of frustration, and the intricate, very strong relationships found between frustration and aggression.

Another theory of aggression, attracting researchers embedded in many separate scientific disciplines (psychology, sociology, anthropology, primatology, and even philosophy), proposed concepts questioning the innate nature of aggression and seeking its sources exclusively in social learning mechanisms. At the same time, these concepts indicated either operant conditioning (learning from consequences or one's own experience through a punishment-and-reward mechanism) or modeling (learning by applying another's experience by observing operating "models") (Bandura, 1973). Numerous studies in this direction, initiated by Albert Bandura, including his famous Bobo doll experiment, generated detailed descriptions of behavior-modeling mechanisms and a solid foundation in the theory of social learning as a concept especially important not only to the issue of aggression but also to a comprehensive spectrum of psychological matters. Despite this resonance, though, this way of conceptualizing the phenomenon of aggression did not produce a comprehensive and fully acceptable concept. It did not decisively reject the arguments of researchers defending the innate nature of aggressive behavior.

Much credit in this respect should be attributed to Fromm, who built his notion of aggression as a concept of human destructiveness in overt opposition and unequivocal objection to the ethological approach (also in contradiction to behavioral explanations).

Applying the tools of Freudian psychoanalysis but without accepting its specific biologism and opposing the concept of the death drive, Fromm tried to point out to the characterological conditions of aggression. In turn, he sought their sources, especially those of characterological deformations, in the fissures of social structures. Conclusively, he believed that a reliable diagnosis of human destructiveness is possible only when reaching into the depths of the social system (Fromm 1973). Moreover, the elimination of human destructiveness is achieved primarily through regulations and appropriate modifications within this system; it is in the system that the conditions for satisfying the most important human needs lie. It is not aggression that is in human nature. The fundamental existential needs are in human nature: the needs for love, creativity, and self-realization, among others. The inability to satisfy them properly is a direct source of aggression (in its "malicious," typically human form)—and satisfying these needs brings hope of eliminating our destructiveness.

In existential analysis and the concept of logotherapy, Viktor Frankl also attributed the sources of human aggression to the sphere of the unmet needs. In his theory, the sublime needs of spiritual nature acquire a fundamental character, completed with the universal need for sense. The propensity for aggression, according to this approach, is correlated with emptiness and existential frustration: aggression thus results from an unmet need for sense, from feeling the lack of sense. The existential vacuum, as stated by Frankl, was an attribute of the 20th century (Frankl 1985) and the origin of the "mass neurotic triad" specific to that time: aggression, addiction, and depression. Nonetheless, aggressiveness, though determined by the specific character of the times, ultimately remains within human competence. As specified by Frankl, humans, with their freedom, rationality, and responsibility, finally decide on aggressiveness. It is spirituality of humans, regardless of the strength of their instinctive impulses and despite the pressure of neurotic times, that shapes human attitudes free from aggression and hostility, and constitutes a kind of resistance to them.

Another perspective disputing the idea that aggression (violence and evil) is inherent in human nature has been presented by theoreticians on the basis of modern neurobiological discoveries. For example, Joachim Bauer (2011) and Simon Baron-Cohen (2011) have proposed especially inspiring resolutions, each, however, representing a decidedly different research line. Notwithstanding these fundamental differences, both concepts intend to "demythologize" and demystify aggression, violence, and evil by revealing their associations with specific neurobiological mechanisms, which are by no means indications of the innate nature of aggression. In Bauer's publications, the phenomena of aggression are closely related to the so-called pain-threshold principle. Its starting point is the key recognition that the human neurobiological motivational system is focused on social acceptance (Bauer 2011). Aggression supports this system as a complementary instrument, a specific signal mechanism triggered in situations threatening us with social exclusion, breaking of social bonds, and loss of social acceptance. These situations, like physical discomfort, gradually lead to the pain threshold, which triggers aggression as a neurobiological, reactive behavior program. In contrast, counteracting and suppressing aggression (or more precisely, as postulated by Bauer, maintaining it at a level that does not exceed its communicative function) is possible due to a wide spectrum of activities limiting the intensity of pain (in the spheres of law, morality, religion, and art) as well as building and strengthening social trust.

Still, in the approach proposed by Baron-Cohen, the phenomenon of aggression and all human cruelty are perceived as "the erosion of empathy" and, therefore, as the effects of abnormalities within "the brain's empathy circuit." Here, the key is that the environmental factors (primarily childhood experiences) interacting with "empathy genes" are responsible for these irregularities to a significant degree (Baron-Cohen 2011). Research conducted by Baron-Cohen within the field known as social neuroscience is aimed at revealing the neurological, genetic, and social conditions determining the level of empathy or the ability to recognize another's thoughts and feelings and respond to them with appropriate emotions. Nonetheless, the aim of the research is to recognize how extremely complex the structure of "the brain's empathy circuit" is and how rich the correlation of the spectrum with the environment is. However, the overriding intention of the research remains to realize that empathy is one of the most valuable resources in our world (Baron-Cohen 2011). And it is essential to multiply this resource to simply "infect with" empathy—we owe it to the victims of cruelty and violence that have swept over human history.

Research developed by Baron-Cohen is one of those projects whose value arises from original, well-established resolutions, interesting and important inspirations, and wise sensitization to the most important problems of the social world. Moreover, the important value of this project, if assessed from the perspective of the question of whether aggression is in human nature, also comes from enabling the realization that the distinctions designated by this question raise increasingly serious reservations. It is ever clearer that, contrary to traditional expectations, these distinctions turn out to be inadequate and inconclusive, raising serious doubts about the legitimacy of the question itself.

Moreover, such suggestions can be drawn from more than Baron-Cohen's theory. In fact, in the whole history of the dispute over aggression, human cruelty, and violence, it has been gradually recognized that there are more and more pronounced symptoms, indicating that whether aggression pertains to human nature is simply a badly posed question. Even though it has spurred a highly important dispute over aggression and has driven the philosophical and ethical discourse devoted to it to the highest levels—along with its anthropological, sociological, psychological, and pedagogical discourses—this question itself is unsuitable. It should not bear the burden of research and debate on aggression. It should not be a matter of our concern. What, though, does its weakness consist of? What is wrong with this question?

Primarily, the question hides in its very sound some very strong, important assumptions with numerous consequences that require just diligent problematization. It assumes that two separate orders determine human behavior (e.g., attitudes, features, and predilections) and that every human characteristic is shaped by only one of these orders: either natural features or socialization processes. These seemingly obvious assumptions are by no means evident. They require detailed consideration, problematization, and recognition of their consequences. Under no circumstances should they be waved aside—because in almost every historically recorded concept of aggression (including those not mentioned here), some doubts and suggestions can be found that, above all, allow for gradually perceiving the presence of these very assumptions and understanding their importance to the ways in which research on aggression is conducted. Moreover, they create opportunities to see the nonobviousness of the assumed distinction, and, finally, they permit the slow construction of a theoretical distance between them. All these circumstances ultimately create opportunities to free research on aggression from the question of whether aggression pertains to human nature. They provide opportunities to subordinate this research to a completely different and, I believe, more important question.

However, this proposed shift in no way devalues the attitudes and resolutions that have historically emerged in the dispute over whether aggression pertains to human nature. Somewhat paradoxically, this false question, this incorrectly formulated problem, does not make the disputes based on it irrelevant and worthless. The misguided question does not necessarily lead to a pointless debate. The history of philosophy shows many situations in which this was not the case. It can almost be said that the strongest, most significant philosophical disputes have taken place based on falsely constructed refinements, incorrectly conceptualized distinctions, and, therefore, inadequately posed questions, yet they have run the machine of philosophical thought with great force. The most prominent examples have been the disputes between empiricism and rationalism, determinism and teleologism, and materialism and idealism; these have taken place in every philosophical field. In almost every field, the driving forces have been debates based on oppositions we know today had no reason to exist. Simultaneously, awareness of the incorrect presentation of the problem, of the inappropriate or even false base distinction, has appeared very slowly and always as the result of persistent disputes. It used to be almost a rule that abandonment of the initial formulation and revision of the initial question could only take place over a long intellectual journey that made the question redundant. It seems that each time a mechanism similar to the Wittgenstein "ladder" worked—it could only be discarded once it was possible to climb to the top. Reason or senses? Cause or purpose? Form or matter? Innate or acquired?—without these overarching questions and fundamental distinctions, two and a half thousand years of history of Western philosophy would not exist. However, at the same time, they are oppositions, and abandoning them has been an indispensable condition for the development of current philosophy.

In relation to research and analyses that make aggression their subject, the current perspective shifts focus to the problem of **co-responsibility**.

Instead of asking whether or to what extent aggression applies to human nature, let us make an effort to answer the question of whether and to what extent we are co-responsible for every single manifestation of human aggression, for the phenomena of violence and cruelty, and for the evil that sweeps through our world. These questions, though fairly pathetic, have a solid theoretical foundation in a well-established social concept and the ethical doctrine organizing it.[3] As such, they absolutely demand the full subordination of every possible theory of aggression to them. Whether it is a theory that exposes the instrumental or reactive nature of aggression, a theory that investigates aggression as a characterological condition or existential frustration, a theory that decodes neurophysiological dependencies, or a theory that conceptualizes aggression as a consequence of the loss of sense—every type of research on aggression can be and, above all, should be correlated and subordinate to the problem of co-responsibility as far as possible. How is it possible from the theoretical point of view? How is the ethical principle of co-responsibility justified? What gives it the rank of a superior ethical and social instance, and how can it be implemented? These issues need to be carefully reconstructed because only thanks to such reconstruction is it possible to validly **embed the problem of aggression in the normative project of social co-responsibility**. Moreover, it is possible to emphasize new content, propose new and different interpretations, and draw new conclusions from almost all historically proposed theories of aggression that definitely lack sensitivity to the perspective of co-responsibility. It is simple to imagine how radically this perspective could remodel the interpretations of the two most famous and still-cited psychological experiments related to the problem of aggression—those of Stanley Milgram (1963) and Philip Zimbardo (2007). Imposing the perspective of social co-responsibility on other theoretical projects regarding aggression should lead to numerous interesting and valuable results.

However, this perspective does not depreciate or reject existing ideas, and in no circumstances does it lead to their complete elimination. Rather, it allows perceiving that the historically proposed theories of aggression (including those previously specified) **complement** one another. Despite the critical edge they usually direct toward one another, even small theoretical endeavors can enable seeing them as complementary, forming a coherent whole, and often providing one another with contexts of justification. Recognizing this complementarity is extremely important because it opens up an opportunity for a systemic, holistic approach to the phenomena of aggression, and it is a *sine qua non* condition for comprehensive, extensive theorization of aggression. It, therefore, creates access to a theory that could guarantee a consistent interpretation of all possible aspects and levels of the constitution of the phenomena of aggression—from the biological, physiological, impulse, and instinctive factors through the social and cultural determinants to the dimensions of sublime spirituality and the existential and metaphysical dilemmas. The multidimensional character of this theory would align as closely as possible with the rich, multidimensional nature of aggression itself.

A specific anticipation of this approach is the General Aggression Model (GAM) proposed in 1995 by a team from the University of Missouri-Columbia (Anderson 1995). This model was constructed based on research showing that violence in the media affects aggressive behavior (and especially stimulates aggressive reactions among children and adolescents). However, the universal character of the model attracted considerable interest, causing it to be included in a much wider debate (stimulated by the references to *The Seville Statement on Violence* (UNESCO 1986)). In the GAM structure, it is especially important to emphasize the interactive nature of two separate classes of the determinants of aggressive reactions: personal (individual) factors and environmental factors. In their interactions can be observed the forces shaping the subject's internal state, which consists of cognitive aspects, affective states, and physiological arousals (bringing to mind the famous Platonic tripartite division of soul). The complex interactions of all these factors determine the display of aggression. In this comprehensive approach lies the greatest value of the GAM, even though it is still relatively narrow in nature, and many relevant measures for the reconstruction of aggression mechanisms remain beyond its reach.

Nevertheless, to restate this very important suggestion, only as the result of such an approach recognizing the complementary nature of all the concepts of aggression proposed so far can we create a chance for a respectable theory: a theory that contains a coherent, comprehensive vision of human aggressiveness and frees reflection on it from fragmentation, bias, and other maladies still restricting our understanding of these severe phenomena. Relating such a theory to social co-responsibility, in turn, offers hope of creating a solid theoretical foundation for real, practical actions that trigger mechanisms to control, regulate, and eliminate aggression—also through effective prevention. Let us believe that they will be so-called "clever" tools given a universal status, just as the ethical principle of co-responsibility remains indisputably universal, as is demonstrated in detail in the following chapters of this book, particularly those devoted to the ethics project. Moreover, the theoretical values of the suggested approach—the approach taking into consideration the complementarity of opinions and the approach embedded in the perspective of the social co-responsibility project—are revealed mainly through the analyses directly related to aggression in the media space.

At this point, some explanation or, rather, a necessary justification still needs to be made. Here, contrary to widespread practice, my analysis of attitudes has not been preceded by any definition or attempt to specify the key category to which these viewpoints relate. There are no proposals on how the term "aggression" should be understood or the meanings attributed to it explained. No suggestions are made; no authorities are indicated. However, this deficiency has not resulted from arrogance or disrespect for academic norms. It has occurred simply because each of the cited opinions and the concepts modeled the content of the term differently and did not necessarily use a precise (or even a similar) definition. This "modeling" took place alongside the analyses, proposed interpretations, and suggested conclusions, and usually was not strongly emphasized. Regardless of what term a given concept applied ("violence," "hostility," "destructiveness," "cruelty," "oppression," and "evil" were often used almost interchangeably or along with "aggression"), the layer of meaning of the term was always constituted as the whole concept was formed; its significance was inherent in the shape of the key resolutions of this concept. Using an overriding, seemingly neutral meaning of the term, therefore, is a rather obvious misuse of it, which complicates rather than facilitates understanding of the phenomena of aggression. Undoubtedly, the charm of definition tempts and attracts, but reliability limits itself to purely colloquial associations—one must always be aware that, however helpful and guiding as to meanings, they are full of ambiguity and confusion.

The same applies to the term "aggression," most often cited in the literature of subject today, according to which, as Robert Baron and Deborah Richardson suggested, it refers to "any form of behavior whose purpose is to cause harm or cause injury to another living being, motivated to avoid such treatment" (Krahé, 2013 p. 17). This is a kind of the understanding of the term we use regularly in language and in popular science and scientific jargon. Roughly, this sense moves through all the concepts of aggression, presenting a good first impression and the first clue to the contexts and circumstances in which the term "aggression" is used. Nonetheless, this understanding of aggression also quickly reveals its limitations and thus requires appropriate modifications. Understanding aggression in the form it takes in the media is a good example.

## Notes

1 The analyses proposed by Steven Pinker (2003), among others, warn in an interesting way about the fears and prejudices that lie behind many contemporary theorists' embrace of the idea of *tabula rasa* as

they obsessively reject even the smallest traces of nativism or any form of biological determinism.
2 The creators of this hypothesis were John Dollard, Neal Miller, Leonard Doob, Orval Mowrer, and Robert Sears.
3 The concept of the communication community and the ethics of co-responsibility project are referred to here.

# 2 The World in the Chains of Megamedia

The scale of aggression observed in the media today is not easy to describe with one theoretical pattern. It is neither simple to diagnose where its strength comes from nor to point to a universal and effective antidote to it. This difficulty arises not only from the above exposed complicated and complex nature of aggression but also from the extremely elaborate, multi-level, and dynamically variable structure of the media space itself. Indeed, its current state seems so confusing that even the most inquisitive researchers have not been able to discern it until recently. It was impossible to imagine the scale in which the media space could overwhelm absolutely all dimensions of our world. Never before have we experienced such a huge addiction to it—both on an individual scale and on a global scale. All the more reason, therefore, that the media space requires close, constant attention. It requires extraordinary attention!

To apply not very theoretical jargon, what we call the "media space" is (in general and still not very precisely) a global complex of media-mediated processes of communication and the relations determined by them. It is the entirety of communication cooperation implemented through the media as well as its multi-faceted results. The way we conceptualize communication is principal to a complete understanding of the specifics of this space. And, contrariwise, the efforts to provide a detailed description of the current shape of media reality allow for a relevant and valuable complement to our understanding of communication in general. This relationship has considerable theoretical value, which is discussed below.

It should be noted, however, that when talking about "media-mediated communication" (or "media communication"), we use a common simplification. By its very nature, communication is always somehow mediated, and various artifacts serve as its medium: a sound, a graphical sign, a musical phrase, and a color system as well as a gesture, a facial expression, and a choreographic routine.

In this sense, communication is always carried out through some medium, and therefore, it is always of a media nature. However, when we use the term "media communication," we do not refer to "communication activity," only to its form, which is implemented through mass media and those that have evolved from mass media, and in terms of significant aspects that have exceeded (or are currently exceeding) their framework. Accordingly, a wide range of meaning applies to the very concept of media.

The eternal dynamics of the media space transformations (depicted in an interesting way by the metaphor of the "media clock" or inspiringly conceptualized as "mediamorphoses" (McQuail 2010; Fidler 1997)) have accelerated spectacularly in recent decades, in an inseparable feedback loop with the processes of globalization. These changes in the technological dimension, which were enabled first by the expansion of analog electronic media, next by the dynamic development of digital media, and finally by the unprecedented "explosion" of mobile media,[1] meant that our existence imperceptibly began to take place in a new, changed reality, which was no longer the reality of the mass media, but what can most aptly be called the **megamedia** world. Today, our media space is the megamedia space, and every feature of this space disclosed confirms the validity of such a definition.

In megamedia reality, most of the characteristics that were associated with mass media coverage, and thus partly with mass media culture, undergo shifts and modifications as well as complications. These are not always radical modifications, as they do not always deal with the cancellation of the most essential features of mass media reality, and yet everything that we experience today is a complete novelty. Although we may not notice such radical novelty and powerful qualitative change, this ultimately entails a shift in our fundamental communication relations and, as a consequence, a new way of embedding humans in the structures of communication.

The detailed characteristics of megamedia communication, as the space constituted both by specific technical means and by new (or modified) forms of communication cooperation, and through the specific products of this cooperation, can be delineated by comparing them with the features of mass media communication as described in the classic publications in the field of mass communication theory (among others: Baran 2002; Goban-Klas 2002; McQuail 2010). These characteristics can be arranged in a fairly transparent set of pairs, in which the first part is an important feature of mass media communication, and the second is a characteristic, or at least clear trend, determining the specifics of megamedia communication. A summary of these pairs can be presented in this way:

1. mass reception versus tendencies for individualization and personalization
2. unidirectionality of the communication relation versus reciprocity and multidimensionality
3. verticality of the communication relation versus its horizontality (and diagonality)
4. "sender–receiver" relation versus participation
5. passive reception versus interactivity
6. linear structure of the transfer versus hypertextual structure
7. conventionality and periodicity of transfer versus randomness and spontaneity
8. distinctiveness of individual media versus media convergence, transmediality, and multimedia
9. separation of production from marketing versus unity of production and marketing
10. institutional production and distribution versus non-institutional commitment
11. expert knowledge versus collective knowledge
12. fourth power versus fifth power

In addition, there are many other specific features and phenomena of the megamedia world, among which the most salient are:

13. unprecedented media ubiquity
14. unprecedented media availability
15. unprecedented equality in access to knowledge and creation
16. unprecedented multiplication and diversity of communication events in the mediasphere

The characteristics and phenomena of megamedia communication summarized here by no means determine the full spectrum of properties and features of today's media world. This list has deliberately omitted almost all the features that are already consequences of the specified changes, namely social, political, ideological, and psychological ones. Also, those characteristics that have a clearly evaluating or assessing meaning have not been included here. Undoubtedly, they are of great importance, both in theoretical and practical terms, but they are derivative of characteristics listed here, and, as such, they require a separate level of analysis.

It is also obvious that this is not a simple, sudden, or one-time change of reality. All shifts that constitute the specifics of the megamedia world are gradually accumulating, which happens at a different, not very synchronized pace. This movement does not facilitate an accurate diagnosis of the phenomenon. Similarly, the fact that these processes are taking place right before our eyes does not facilitate such a diagnosis, and, therefore, when conceptualizing these processes, we lack the theoretical "comfort" that an adequate temporal distance can provide. Here, Minerva's owl must change its habits.

The analyses of the phenomena and features that comprise the megamedia communication space and determine the character of the modern world are scattered throughout the publications of numerous researchers. These analyses are derived from various theoretical perspectives and therefore indicate different consequences. They also often involve extremely different evaluations. Their synthetic list (and comparison) would undoubtedly give a very interesting and theoretically inspiring picture of today's mediasphere, and, above all, reveal how its character is extraordinarily complicated, heterogeneous, and full of internal tensions, even contradictions. Here, I cannot undertake such a widespread task; nevertheless, even a general view of the listed phenomena allows for an understanding of the scale and extent of the transformations taking place while also indicating their exceptional rank.

Although the characteristics of megamedia communication presented here are rarely observed in their pure or full form, and they often only signal a given tendency or are only a partial feature of new media constellations, they gradually and collectively form a different nature of the mediasphere and consequently bring significant modifications to the sociosphere.

What exactly is this novelty? What makes this new nature stand out? The answer, formulated in the simplest way, sounds seemingly not very convincing, or perhaps even ridiculous: it is only today's mediasphere, as the mega-mediasphere, that opens the space for **real communication cooperation**. In other words, it is only in megamedia reality that the conditions for real communication can form, that is, the way we communicate in everyday life outside mass media tools. Thus, it is the reality that constitutes our specifically human social being, our communication community, and our identity as *homo communicativus*.

The reverse of this diagnosis is the indication (at first glance equally hard to accept) that reality of mass media significantly prevented real communication cooperation, or at least strongly hindered it and certainly always deformed it.

Both the diagnosis proposed here and its contrast presuppose a specific (and quite special) understanding of **communication**. They assume an approach that finds expression in the full complexity of events, processes, and communication relations, including the multiplicity of their aspects and the variety of functions performed. It is an approach that reflects the effects of the communicative research carried out on many different theoretical levels and in many separate scientific disciplines.[2] As a result of such a synthesizing approach, it can be proposed that

> communication is co-intentionally shaped and figuratively mediated cooperation in regulating behaviors, shaping and maintaining social bonds, expression transfer, exchanging information, evoking sensations and emotions, and co-shaping norms, knowledge and social institutions.

An absolutely crucial point of this definition is to clarify communication as a joint, reciprocal action—a special kind of social cooperation.

This special, even extraordinary, nature of **communication cooperation**, and, thus, the fact that it definitely stands out from other human activities, is mainly due to the fact that it is an activity shaped co-intentionally and figuratively mediated—largely mediated by the natural language with its dual, performative, and propositional structure (Searle 1969; Apel 1973; Austin 1976; Habermas 1981; Tomasello 1999). This special character of communication cooperation results in influential consequences in all dimensions of human existence, ultimately determining the characteristics of human culture and our unique social competences. In relation to cogitation limited only to communication processes, it is important that this results in ethical obligations, ultimately culminating in the ethical principle of co-responsibility. Also crucial is that it forces the rigor of discursiveness (understood as the indispensable competence and openness of the participants of the communication process to constantly problematize the legitimacy of the commitments and standards that condition the possibility of communication cooperation).

The proposed formula also indicates (to be very brief again)[3] that what lies at the root of communication processes as social cooperation is the **communication relation**, and this has very serious consequences for all communication processes. It is true that the communication relation can only take place due to the specific competences of the participants involved,[4] but, in fact, it is only this relation that enables the constitution of the subjects of cognition as communication subjects and that constructs these subjects, with their reciprocal obligations and duties, as well as with respected norms and rules. All these factors condition each other in a specific movement of reciprocal references, defining ultimately the framework in which real communication cooperation takes place. Among the obligations and duties, which arise directly from the structure of the communication relation and which, due to the fundamental nature of this relation, unconditionally take effect, there are requirements of equal partnership, reciprocity and equivalence of actions, exchangeability of roles, reciprocal recognition of coherence and decision-making freedom, reciprocal trust regarding truthfulness and meaningfulness, as well as reciprocal trust in possessed communication competences (both semantic and pragmatic). Equally rigorous is the complexity of the norms implied by the structure of the communication relation, norms that retain an ethical nature and whose final culmination is the principle of co-responsibility.[5]

Finally, it is decisive that the proposed formula for communication takes into consideration the extremely wide and rich scope in which it is implemented (from expression transfer to co-shaping social institutions), and that, as I have already mentioned, and which is discussed later in the book, many of the basic **functions** of communication (as well as many of its fundamental properties) are already determined by the very formal structure of the communication relation.[6]

All these circumstances are, at the same time, the main traces that suggest that the conditions imposed on communication processes by mass media from the very beginning significantly limited, deformed, or even prevented real communication (as social cooperation in the aforementioned sense). This suggestion seems to be confirmed by each of the characteristics indicated in the mass media and megamedia communication clash presented above as well as by each of the phenomena revealed in this confrontation.

Even with a cursory look at the individual points in the presented set, it is easy to notice that the changes in today's media space, which are gradually transforming it into the mega-mediasphere, are shaping in a completely new way the nature of relations and therefore communication processes. This transformation in relations is gradually allowing for the full implementation of communication cooperation in the mediasphere, and as a consequence, it seems to herald very important but also very complicated changes within the sociosphere.

In particular, the first five points of the proposed comparison deal with phenomena of extraordinary importance for the ongoing transformation. The individualization and personalization of media coverage, its reciprocal and multidimensional nature, the horizontal aspect of the communication relation, and the shifts from the static nature of "sender–receiver" and passive receptivity in favor of participation and interactivity are all trends that make the megamedia space gradually open to real communication cooperation. This new and evolving media space creates the conditions enabling this cooperation, which means that it provides the opportunity to disclose and to "activate" all the obligations, claims, norms, and duties that are inscribed in the structure of the communication relation and which set the boundary conditions for its implementation.[7] Thus, it opens the field of communication for the implementation of all its functions (from expression transfer to co-shaping social institutions). Concisely, the megamedia space becomes the space of real communication cooperation.

Against this background, it is possible to observe that mass media communication, determined by the mass reception, unidirectionality, and vertical aspects of the communication relation, by the rigorous separation of the roles of sender and receiver and the resulting inaction in the reception process, could not ensure and has never ensured the conditions for real communication. This new "shape" of the media space, gradually resulting in full communication cooperation, is overlapped (at an incredibly fast pace and with staggering results) by the phenomena listed in the last four points of the proposed comparison: namely, the unprecedented ubiquity of media; the unprecedented availability of media; the unprecedented equality of access to knowledge and creation; and the unprecedented multiplication and diversity of communication events in the mediasphere. All these phenomena are associated with the fact that the processes of communication, which are already common, simply "transfer" to the media space (the strongest example of which is obviously today's political life; however, this situation equally applies to many other spheres of everyday life, including financial and business transactions; social and professional commitments; artistic and scientific activity; medical, matrimonial, educational, and even pastoral services, not to mention the various forms of criminal activity). And, even if, in a given area, such "transfer" does not take place or remains only partial, the communication processes taking place within it lose their independence from the mediasphere, in the sense that the ever-widening spectrum of patterns, norms, and standards operating in that particular area has its real source in this mediasphere.

Therefore, the nature of today's mediasphere, very different from that constituted by mass media communication, is formed by both the radically different characteristics of communication relations that define it (the characteristics described by the other points of the aforementioned comparison) and an absolutely new scale of media phenomena that have never been experienced before, along with new forms of participation in the media space and a degree of involvement in it that still surprises us (not yet fully recognizable in all its consequences). It is the total nature of these phenomena, their almost unlimited range and overwhelming impact that prompted—in looking for a term that would accurately reflect their extraordinary scale and importance—the term "megamediality." Therefore, in relation to today's reality, we can talk about megamedia, megamedia communication, the megamedia space, and even the megamedia world.

It is essential that "megamediality" is not only a descriptive category but also a "diagnostic," critical, and (as far as possible) predictive one. Certainly in all these aspects it is, as has already been indicated, in significant (though "changeable") opposition to mass media phenomena.

Among other things, megamediality has, in an interesting way, a critical aspect in contrast to such (intensively exposed in the era of mass media) terms as "information society," "information age," "information capitalism," and "information infrastructure." Since the 1960s, these terms precisely reflected the spirit of the times. So much so that, by the 1990s, they had been incorporated into influential scientific theories (e.g., Castells 1998) as well as reflected in a number of official documents of national and international importance[8] as the expression of the unquestioned power of mass media, in their technological, economic, and institutional dimensions. However, confronted with the megamedia space, these terms are also a testimony of the extreme extent to which the communication implemented in the mass media space limits the spectrum of its possible functions, by focusing exclusively or primarily on the information function to the detriment of other functions. Among these, the phatic function, which is understood as the shaping and maintaining of social bonds, suffers the most serious damage, but the knowledge-creating function, which seems to be undergoing irreversible deformation under the pressure of powerful political and financial interests, is becoming equally problematic and complex. Thomas Eliot, in his famous sententia, asked with concern: "Where is the wisdom we have lost in knowledge? Where is the knowledge we have lost in information?" (Eliot 1934). This is an accurate and serious statement. However, the monopoly of information proved to be much more powerful than Eliot recognized. Due to mass media, the omnipotence of information has eliminated from the communication space, or effectively overshadowed, the entire spectrum of phenomena and properties inherently coupled with the human communication activity and ultimately conditioning it.[9] In other words, it has eliminated the factors that were essential to it.

The ultimate effect of these reductions in communication functions is not only the severe and highly dangerous phenomena within the mediasphere but also the severe narrowing of the understanding of interpersonal communication processes and even a common misunderstanding of what, in fact, communication is. The primary and privileged role of the information function and its feedback loop with the strengthening of media imperialism consistently reinforce the belief that the transfer of information (not even its exchange) is the essence of the communication processes taking place among people—that the transfer of information (regardless of its nature and the circumstances determining it) is the superior goal, intention, and task appropriate for all communication processes, whether performed in the media space or outside of it.

This way of perceiving the communication processes is unquestionably negligible in terms of real communication cooperation and gives us only a small degree of access to its proper understanding. It allows us to trace many complex and important phenomena that are characteristic of mass media activity but ultimately makes us helpless in facing the magnitude of the various types of problems caused by the overflow of infomass and the deliberate development of the entire infosphere and the unexpected consequences that surprise us with new media constellation in the form of megamediality. Moreover, the phenomena of aggression observed in this space—phenomena experienced in many forms and as ubiquitous as media today—are particularly serious consequences that require an absolutely decisive response.

## Notes

1 Each stage of these successive technological "revolutions" generated significant changes in the functioning of existing forms of media communication and initiated the creation of numerous, completely new forms. Some of these novelties manage to maintain a relatively stable position, and others—for various reasons—have disappeared from the media space. Today, the most "solidified" are various web portals, blogs and mini blogs, as well as Wikipedia, YouTube, Facebook, Instagram, Snapchat, Twitter, and TikTok.
2 The directions and inspiration of this research are presented in more detail in Chapters 4 and 5.
3 More about this aspect in Chapters 4 and 5. The necessity to refer to further parts of the book is a consequence of the "spiral" structure of the considerations. This, in turn, is forced by the specificity of the project of transcendental pragmatics, in which each of the main categories refers to the full categorial structure. Thus, explication of these categories needs to be of a relational nature, which means that certain categories and theoretical relationships can be fully explained only in further parts of the text.
4 The question about these competences seems to be the main subject of the research concern of Michael Tomasello, who (in a strictly late Wittgensteinian spirit) penetrates human cognitive and communication processes in a particularly inquisitive and conclusive manner, in a significant part in terms of the co-intentionality and motivation to cooperate that condition them.
5 As it is presented in Chapter 8.
6 The findings in this regard made in the transcendental pragmatics of Karl-Otto Apel and the universal pragmatics of Jürgen Habermas are discussed in Chapter 6.
7 The conditions and properties of communication cooperation resulting from the formal structure of the communication act itself are discussed in Chapters 4 and 6.
8 For example, *National Information Infrastructure* (an American document from 1991); *Europe and the Global Information Society: Recommendations to the European Council* (the so-called Bangemann Report from 1994); *eEurope—An Information Society for All* (a project of European Commission from 1999); *eEurope 2002: An Information Society for All. Action Plan* (a document from 2000).
9 The factors conditioning the communication processes are presented in Chapters 4 and 5.

# 3 Aggression in the Megamedia World

The scale of phenomena implied by the total, rapid, and unstoppable development of megamedia communication gradually makes megamedia the essential characteristic of the contemporary world. Although it does not make the existing mass media constellations completely disappear or change radically, it creates a new reality that brings not only new opportunities and new possibilities[1] but also new (or at least modified) problems and dangers.

Among the **negative phenomena**, which include aggression, there are those transferred into the world of media simply from the real world; however, there are also many that (partially or exclusively) owe their existence to those forms of communication that are specific to the megamedia space.[2]

Those that arouse the greatest concern (sometimes even hysterical) seem to refer to three extremely important spheres—disproportionate, admittedly, in their scope and not always separate but clearly distinguishable. These are phenomena that pose a threat, first, to the sphere of security (in various fields and with varying intensity); second, to the sphere of freedom (in various scopes and with a broad understanding of freedom); and, third, to the sphere of human dignity (also in its various meanings). These threats are both individual and supra-individual, and their strength is, to a large extent, enhanced by the domination of two powerful but new and long-thwarted tendencies: namely, the politicization and commercialization of almost all aspects of our lives. Interestingly, both these tendencies have found exceptionally fertile ground for their own development in the megamedia space, "improving" at an extremely fast pace, and, at the same time, creating significant transformations both in politics and business, as well as in numerous other areas.

All these circumstances unfortunately translate into an extensive and varied map of painful, dangerous, and difficult phenomena with which the world of megamedia is struggling: phenomena that, on the one hand, reciprocally stimulate and complement one another, and, on the other hand, fit into trends that are often contradictory and incompatible with one another. Their negative consequences are of many kinds: from the psychological, social, and cultural to the economic, political, and ideological as well as the medical or biological.

In the research and literature on the subject, the most severe, and therefore those requiring the greatest social care, include such phenomena as the intrusiveness of the media message (Krzysztofek 2013), surveillance (e.g., dataveillance (Schneier 2015), phishing (Jagatic 2007), enslavement by incomprehensible technology (Castells 2001), biased aggregation and gatekeeping (McCombs 2004; Battelle 2005; Shoemaker 2009), cyberhoaxes (Castells 2001), the crisis of privacy (Van Dijk 2006), the drastic tabloidization of public life (Sparks 2000), the mixing and confusing of the virtual world with reality (Levinson 2009), the weakening of authority (Van Dijk 2006), the impossibility of removing internet content (Mayer-Schönberger 2009), trolling (Cheng 2017), multitasking (Small 2008), the phenomenon of distraction (Crawford 2015), online piracy (Fisk 2009), internet addiction (Young 1998), FOMO (Fear of Missing Out; Przybylski 2013), cybersex (Cooper 2002), online sexual activities (OSA; Shaughnessy 2017), grooming (Pollack 2015), stalking (Haron 2010), and others, as well as various traditional criminal or risky activities supported, and often "ingeniously" modified, with megamedia communication tools (e.g., commercial and business frauds, terrorism, pedophilia, gambling, etc.).

The concern and anxiety caused by such a wide, and yet only randomly exemplified here, range of negative phenomena of the megamedia space, as well as the awareness of a frighteningly wide spectrum of their consequences, have prompted a significant number of studies, undertaken in almost all the social sciences disciplines and in many other fields of science and even art. These studies explain the investigated phenomena in a multi-perspective and detailed way, show where to look for an antidote, and suggest a number of valuable solutions. However, at the same time, they make it clear that none of these phenomena—even the most drastic and traumatic in their consequences—reaches the foundations of social existence and threatens to destroy its deepest structure.

The only negative phenomenon in the megamedia space of which this cannot be said is aggression.[3] **Aggression**, in its complex nature and in its clash with the complicated reality of the megamedia world, is a truly exceptional force. It is still hardly noticeable that within the new space defined by megamedia communication, aggression not only threatens the security, freedom, and dignity of its addressees but also leads to the undermining of the very foundations of communication cooperation and threatens to destroy the inalienable conditions of its possibilities.[4] Thus, aggression is becoming an exceptionally serious threat to social reality that is "underestimated" in its gravity. This is occurring despite the fact that on a global scale, as diagnosed by Steven Pinker (2011), acts of traditional aggression and all the manifestations of violence that have been observed in the history of humankind lose their strength, frequency, and intensity over time. Paradoxically, aggression, which, in the real world today, has much milder and less frequent manifestations than it had during the millennia of human civilization, becomes, under the conditions of megamedia, a threat of the highest level, a threat reaching the very essence of our social existence. It is, in fact, a threat that puts us on the brink of disaster!

However, the gravity of this situation has emerged very slowly. Even to this day, the belief in the destructiveness of media aggression, which has been repeatedly announced and has stimulated innumerable theoretical and practical achievements in various contexts, is rarely accompanied by a full awareness of the severity of the problem and the scope of its consequences. Although admittedly, in most cases, this does not diminish the accuracy of the proposed detailed solutions or undermine the explanatory efforts, it strongly dampens the radical approach that this issue absolutely requires and does not offer a systemic and comprehensive approach to it.

The beginnings of the research on media aggression date back to the mid-1990s, the years during which the expansion of megamedia was initiated. Very quickly, these studies began to cover its various aspects and, as such, began to be situated within many separate scientific disciplines—especially the pedagogical sciences, with the powerful contribution of psychology, sociology, political, the legal and medical sciences, and the involvement of media experts and people directly active in the world of media (e.g., Butler 1997; Toulouse 1998; Berners-Lee 1999; Suler 2004; Kowalski 2012; Pyżalski 2012; Cicchirillo 2015; Krumsiek 2017; Bauman 2019).

What is intriguing is that many recognized and valuable works (also of a textbook nature) presenting comprehensive theories of the media space and media society (e.g., Baran 2002; Van Dijk 2006; Levinson 2009; McQuail 2010) have almost silently passed over the issues of aggressive and violent attitudes and behavior in the mediasphere. Even if these issues appeared in these studies, they concerned only the influence of aggression coming from media screens on the attitudes, behaviors, and emotions of receivers (mainly children and adolescents) and usually concluded that there was no reliable research that could clearly explain these relationships.

In fact, this relationship remains ambiguous, despite the fact that such research is increasingly carried out, and it often applies to adults and covers newer media areas. A problem that is particularly evident in the research today is the violence and aggression exhibited by computer games. This investigation centers on the questions of how this confrontation can be beneficial for us, to what extent it is disastrous, and how exactly it affects the individual aspects of our life (Ferguson 2008).

A separate, very extensive area of research today pertains to peer media aggression: those attitudes and behaviors witnessed among children and adolescents, which more and more often occur outside the school environment. Undoubtedly, this research is significantly influenced by the intensity of media aggression among children and young people (who, as "digital natives" (Prensky 2001), employ megamedia tools for their purposes with particular ease), with the aim of developing effective educational means to prevent and counteract this aggression. As part of this research, the phenomena of aggression are explored in their full range and variety, taking into consideration all their possible consequences. It is especially valuable that comprehensive, international research projects are devoted to these phenomena; large-scale social programs are initiated; and many different specialists are involved in their implementation. This clearly shows how important and serious the phenomenon of media aggression has become (not only for children and adolescents) and that it requires a comprehensive diagnosis, thorough systemic explanations and "tight" decisive preventive actions implemented with the utmost consistency. Only research with an interdisciplinary scope, brought together on a solidly established theoretical basis, can fully accomplish this. The task of constructing such necessary foundations of knowledge (whether interdisciplinary or maintaining rigorous discipline divisions) has traditionally belonged to philosophy, especially of the Kantian provenance. In this case, philosophy should be consistently faithful to this tradition.

In its long history, however, philosophy has rarely focused on the issue of aggression in the sphere of interpersonal communication, mainly because it did not have the appropriate theoretical tools to do that. The specific exclusion of linguistic communication practices, characteristic of European philosophical thought (resulting from several theoretical "decisions" specific to it, still grounded in the conclusions of ancient Greek philosophy), also naturally deterred questions about communicative aggression. It definitely made it impossible to notice this problem and integrate it into the constructed theories. This situation changed, however, with the emergence of a new (and, as for this science, still very young today) philosophical subdiscipline—the **philosophy concerning communication**.[5] From this perspective, the explanation of the structures and mechanisms that determine communication cooperation has created a solid theoretical basis for the conceptualization of the phenomena of aggression in the communication sphere in general and therefore within megamedia communication. It has also created the possibility of an adequate and comprehensive assessment of the rank of this problem.

However, a philosophical theory maintains its explanatory and justifying power only through its reference to the specific constellations in the social space. Their arrangement in the case of megamedia aggression (as aggressive attitudes and behaviors, manifested and implemented with the use of modern technologies specific to megamedia communication) is exceptionally extensive, multifaceted, and varied. The grasping of this arrangement and even partial ordering of the phenomena of megamedia aggression is supported by numerous **typological** suggestions, which can be complemented by initially establishing the very criteria according to which it is possible to distinguish these phenomena.

In this respect, there are at least four relatively unambiguous and clear **criteria** that allow for differentiating the acts of media aggression. These criteria distinguish such acts according to (1) the addressee of the aggression, (2) form of aggression, (3) type of medium mediating the act of aggression, and (4) methods and tools used to carry out a given act of aggression.

These criteria allow, for example, the grouping of acts of aggression in the following order:

- due to the **addressee** of aggression, for instance:
  - familiar people, strangers, public figures
  - peer, professional, social, or age groups
  - people of a specific nationality or who identify with a specific subculture

- groups with specific political, ideological, religious, sexual, aesthetic preferences, and so on
- people with a specific social status and physical and/or psychological characteristics
- completely undefined addressees (accidental or unimportant for the perpetrator)
• due to the **form** of aggression,[6] for instance:
  - flaming (including threatening, denigration, using hate speech and shaming, etc.)
  - harassment (including bullying)
  - outing and trickery
  - exclusion
  - impersonation
  - cyberstalking
  - sexting (including cyber grooming)
  - happy slapping
• due to the **kind of medium** mediating acts of aggression, for instance:
  - traditional media (mostly digitized and subject to convergence)
  - blogs and miniblogs (together with discussion)
  - forums—mainly provided by internet portals
  - chats
  - social media applications available online (e.g., YouTube, Snapchat, Twitter, Instagram, Facebook, TikTok),
  - instant messengers
  - e-mail
  - mobile phone
• due to the **methods and tools** applied when implementing a given act of aggression, for instance:
  - creating and posting aggressive materials in the media (e.g., videos, blogs, comments on forums, websites, and portals)
  - sending messages (and possibly manipulating them)—flood, bombing
  - fake news
  - deepfake
  - hacking
  - distributing computer viruses
  - cracking[7]

This is not a separable order and division (it does not seem justified to require a typology to be partible); nevertheless, distinguishing these criteria can make the comprehensive typology of megamedia aggression thorough (and this should be a requirement of any typology). As such, it can facilitate both theoretical and practical efforts to develop the tools and methods to combat media aggression, to prevent it, and perhaps even predict it.

There are two other particularly important groups of factors, due to which acts of media aggression (as well as acts of traditional aggression) differ; however, they do not guarantee such unambiguity and transparency of divisions. These are the criteria differentiating aggression due to (1) the **topic** of the act of aggression, either real or constituting only an excuse for it, and due to (2) the **reasons and/or aims** controlling this act, in a more or less aware way. The trouble is, however, that the list of topics, reasons, and aims related to acts of media aggression is almost endless: every topic (from metaphysical abstraction to the specifics of everyday life) and every reason (from undisputed universal and serious to meticulously particular, trivial, or frivolous) today can be the trigger or the driving force behind aggressive attitudes. However, despite this, distinguishing and grouping the most important and frequently recurring topics of acts of aggression, as well as classifying them according to the reasons and aims behind them, are necessary in any attempt to conceptualize these phenomena and as the basis for any actions aimed at them, both those of a diagnostic and preventive nature, and those struggling with the consequences of the phenomena.

The map of megamedia aggression, structured on the basis of the criteria listed here, allows us first to see the complex nature of the phenomenon we are facing, the parameters and dimensions that comprise it, and the scale of difficulty involved in the next stages of completing this picture. The necessity of a wide interdisciplinary approach becomes clear immediately; this is frequently and willingly declared but very difficult to implement (and a special role in its implementation should be entrusted, as mentioned previously,[8] to the philosophical perspective). Finally, the question also arises of how aggression observed in the megamedia space differs from the forms of aggression outside the media environment, which the literature refers to as "traditional aggression."

The topic of the **differences and similarities** of both types of aggression appears regularly in research and scientific discussions. Nevertheless, this matter is far from unanimous, and, above all, there is still no reliable and exhaustive research that would allow for a credible and final answer in this regard. Numerous researchers emphasize the significant similarity of both types of acts and the participation of the same people in them, but they also notice

## Aggression in the Megamedia World 35

the difficulties in transferring the findings and characteristics from one area to another or even emphasize the unique nature of the phenomena related to media-mediated aggression (e.g., Sourander 2010; Olweus 2012; Pyżalski 2012; Kowalski 2014). At the same time, there is a certain set of characteristics that are believed to determine the uniqueness of media aggression, around which fundamental discussion takes place.

A particularly relevant feature in this context is the **anonymity** of the perpetrator (most often the anonymity of an internet nickname), which is observed to have a definitely strengthening impact on the level of manifested aggression (Christopherson 2007; Bernstein 2011; Zimmerman 2014; Shepherd 2015). Such anonymity is associated with the phenomenon of deindividuation (Diener 1980; Postmes 1998; Lee 2007) and the disinhibition effect, which are very much characteristic of electronic aggression (Joinson 1998; Suler 2004). For example, the feature of anonymity has a leading role in enhancing manifestations of hate speech (Shepherd 2015). Anonymity, deindividuation, and disinhibition constitute, as the research seems to reveal, a kind of "electronic cap of invisibility," from under which streams of hate speech flow freely, stimulating universal media aggression to the highest degree.

A phenomenon related to anonymity is the situation referred to as the "**cockpit effect**" (Heirman 2008), which also significantly increases the aggression of megamedia-mediated behavior. The decisive factor in this case is the reduction in the empathy of the perpetrator. The victim is invisible, and, therefore, destructive actions, such as "firing" injuring "bullets" in the form of texts, sounds, and images, are not inhibited by the perpetrator's compassion in response to the victim's reaction. On the other hand, postponed satisfaction with effective aggressive action drives further destructive actions on the part of the perpetrator. Researchers referring to this phenomenon are clear about its role in stimulating aggression.

The situation is slightly different from another circumstance that has been recognized as important in the context of media aggression, which affects not so much the level, frequency, or intensity of aggressive actions but their effectiveness. Numerous studies indicate the **"unsinkability"** of the content that finds its way into the megamedia space and warn against its "eternal" memory (Mayer-Schönberger 2009). It is said, somewhat metaphorically but fully correctly, that "the web does not forget" (and therefore does not forgive). Closely related to this is the phenomenon of the universal and permanent availability of both the object (victim) of aggression and the act of aggression itself. Ultimately, the megamedia space does not give the chance for any asylum, and it does not allow the victim to "take a break." Its aggressive weapon is always ready and strikes without any time and space restrictions.

Finally, megamedia aggressiveness is also fostered by various other minor phenomena that result from breaking communication cooperation from natural, non-media (or it would be more appropriate to say pre-media) reality and cause communication to encounter various types of **disruptions and obstacles** (Bolton 1979). These communication misunderstandings are related to the fact that in media-mediated communication, its context often becomes disturbed and illegible, as it lacks natural feedback, such that there is a limited or distorted emotional message. Moreover, the entire process is often strongly flattened as a result of the reduction to a purely verbal dimension (although non-verbal communication gradually "comes to the fore" even in situations that were traditionally associated only with the written word).

All these factors, namely anonymity, the "cockpit effect," the impossibility of removing the media content, as well as communication obstacles and barriers, undoubtedly significantly increase aggressiveness in the megamedia space, enhance its effects, and foster involvement in aggressive relations and communication behavior. Nonetheless, the question of whether these factors make electronic aggression distinct and fundamentally different from its traditional forms remains. Or is it simply possible to speak of the various proportions of these characteristics and their different distribution?

The Polish scientist Jacek Pyżalski (2012), who was for many years intensely involved in theoretical and empirical research on cyberbullying, proposed the ABACUS theory, which allows for clear comparisons and reciprocal references of these two types of aggression. The fundamental (and important for the debate) conclusion of this theory is that there is, in fact, no distinctive feature that can be attributed solely to electronic aggression, as each of the characteristics commonly associated with aggression and violence observed in the media space to some extent also accompanies traditional aggression. The differences are at best quantitative, and, in qualitative terms, they practically disappear. It is therefore quite clear that they should not be the focus of the main research.

Conforming with this conclusion, it should be noted that the crux of the matter is that the strength of electronic aggression, its destructive "force," and the scale of mutilation suffered by the communication community are influenced not so much by its distinctive features (those characteristics that would clearly distinguish electronic aggression from its traditional forms) as by the **specific nature of the media space** in which these acts of aggression take place. It is all these features that define the specificity of megamedia communication, which ultimately give this form of aggression its extraordinary force of destruction. Predominantly, this results from the fact that, due to these features of megamedia in today's world, virtual reality has become the real space for communication, and the functioning of the real communication community transfers into a dimension aptly described by Paul Levinson as "real virtuality." In addition to this, there are other, extremely important structural shifts, including those that determine the conditions for the possibility of communication cooperation in general. And it is in the most fundamental dimension—the dimension that determines the formal framework of every relationship and every communication event. However, although the role of this dimension is so fundamental, it is not easy to identify and not obvious, either to the participants of communication processes or to the researchers of these processes. Revealing this level as a fundamental one is a special task, requiring the involvement of specific philosophical tools, the basic one here undoubtedly being the procedure of "strict reflexivity" developed within the transcendental-pragmatic project of communication philosophy.[9] Only the findings of communication philosophy, confronted and correlated with the research conducted, among others, within psychology, sociology, and evolutionary anthropology,[10] which allow for the diagnosis of the scale of the threat that results from aggressive and violent behaviors in the megamedia space (even if they seem incidental or not too severe). Above all, these findings allow us to recognize that aggression spreading in the megamedia space is not simply one of the many troubles of the modern, civilized world; to put it a bit metaphorically, it "corrupts" the deepest layer of the social fabric. It destroys the fundamental conditions for the possibility of communication cooperation on a scale imposed by its megamedia dimension and threatens communication with irreversible mutilation and, consequently, total dysfunction.

# Notes

1 Reflection and empirical research on these phenomena, anticipated as early as in the 1990s in the first comprehensive theories of network society (e.g., Castells 1998; Van Dijk 2006), are extremely broad in scope,

and with the spectacular transformations that megamedia communication is undergoing constantly, they are still full of new theories and inspiring "discoveries."
2 See endnote 1 in Chapter 2.
3 Aggression, as a category related to aggressive attitudes, behaviors, and communication activities observed in the megamedia space, is sometimes referred to as network aggression, cyber-aggression, electronic aggression, virtual aggression, or internet aggression. In a general perspective, it can also be referred to as media aggression, and due to the diagnosed shape of today's media, the term "megamedia aggression" becomes the most appropriate. However, the greatest doubts are raised by the term "virtual aggression," as this type of aggression is not so virtual anymore but has become painfully real.
4 These relations are presented in Chapter 4.
5 Its transcendental-pragmatic project is the subject of the following chapter.
6 Most of the forms of cyber-aggression listed here were compiled by Nancy Willard (2007) in the taxonomy she proposed.
7 The last two points are indicated by Pyżalski (2012, 2012a) as "technical aggression."
8 See Introduction.
9 The transcendental-pragmatic procedure of strict reflection is presented in Chapter 6.
10 The main points of such a confrontation are outlined in Chapter 5.

# Part II
# Communication Philosophy

# 4 Communicative *A Priori*

Just as there is no doubt that manifestations of aggression in the megamedia space require the theoretical and empirical involvement of many separate scientific fields and disciplines, it should not be ignored that philosophy plays a special role here, as it does in many other problem areas. The history of the relations linking philosophy with specific fields of science has taken an intriguing course since ancient times, and its twists and turns have often formed surprising constellations. The position of philosophy among the sciences related to the sphere of communication proves to be equally interesting and extremely important. Indeed, the involvement of philosophy in grappling with these issues is considerable in terms of understanding the phenomena of media aggression.

The variety of philosophical opinions relating to the sphere of communication is manifested to the same extent as it is in relation to any other issue that philosophy explores. Today's researchers are looking for significant resolutions concerning interpersonal communication in the majority of significant philosophical theories. Since each case deals with a different theoretical project (Mangion 2011; Chang 2012), the presentation of even the most important of these projects would be quite extensive. However, as regards the question of aggression and violence in communication, the explanation of the fundamental difference between the two main and essentially distinct ways of practicing philosophy reflecting on communication is much more important than presenting a whole range of such opinions.

Similarly to the opposition once proposed by John Searle, namely the "philosophy of language – linguistic philosophy" (Searle 1969), here, we primarily point to the distinction between the "philosophy of communication" and the "communication philosophy" and, in this distinction, recognize the opposition between the distinguished subject of philosophy and its distinguished method.[1]

What does the suggested distinction concern? What are these two separate forms of philosophical reflection on communication? The first, the philosophy of communication, is a subdiscipline of philosophy distinguished due to its specific **subject**. It is therefore a discipline that uses classical philosophical tools to study a distinguished sphere, which comprises communication processes and phenomena. This type of philosophy is a subdiscipline that is situated next to other objectively distinguished philosophical subdisciplines, such as the philosophy of man, philosophy of religion, philosophy of art, and philosophy of law. At the same time, this philosophy successfully competes or effectively cooperates in an interdisciplinary symbiosis with a non-philosophical reflection on communication, including, for example, psychology, sociology, or media studies.

In contrast, the formula of philosophy defined as a "communication philosophy," which is simply characterized by a specific **method**, a specific way of approaching philosophical research in general, is definitely different from the philosophy of communication. It is philosophy in which the main theoretical message obliges us to conceptualize all classical issues of an ontological, epistemological, and ethical nature (to mention only the classical trinity of philosophical subdisciplines) by means of their inalienable involvement in the sphere of communication and with the use of specific theoretical and communication tools. This directive stems precisely from the recognition, fundamental for this philosophy, that the communicative dimension is situated at the very foundations of social existence; sets the framework for the constitution of knowledge; determines the content of normative systems; and, consequently, gains importance in all other spheres covered by philosophical reflection. Communication philosophy, as an original way of philosophical thinking, opens new interpretative horizons, proposing a new paradigm of practicing philosophy that is definitely distinct from the "mentalist paradigm" that dominated in philosophy from modern times to the 20th century (Martens 1985), but it is also clearly modified, compared to the linguistic approach.

The first type of philosophical reflection on communication, gradually taking shape as a subdiscipline of philosophy distinguished by its subject, has a fairly wide representation, and due to its embeddedness in various philosophical concepts and systems, it suggests a wide range of perspectives in which communication phenomena can be conceptualized and provides many inspiring resolutions concerning even the tiniest aspects (Kelly 1981; Cook 2008; Craig 2008). However, there are generally no comprehensive concepts of the communication space, and the relations and processes it comprises are usually perceived as one of many (more or less important) dimensions of reality being reflected.

We face a different approach in the case of the second type of theoretical constructions, that is, those based on the thesis that the communicative dimension is the axis around which subsequent layers of conceptualized reality are built, and that reality itself in its basic features is fully determined by the specificity of relations and communication processes. Such a perspective requires precise theoretical clarifications with regard to all the aspects of communication, and, at the same time, it requires the construction of a comprehensive philosophical concept in which the theoretical and communication tools would allow for explication of all traditional philosophical issues. These requirements quite rigorously determine the final shape of the developed philosophical theories, and the most important theoretical "profit" is the fact that their fulfillment enables philosophical research to cover many very important, but "strange" issues that were previously unavailable to philosophy, including the phenomena of megamedia aggression.

However, not every philosophical project that attempts to construct such a particular theoretical perspective is able to fully and consistently implement these requirements. Most of all, hardly any projects adopt a philosophical attitude so radical as to allow for a complete and credible diagnosis of our communication condition, also in terms of megamedia aggression.

Among those few that have opted for such radicalism, there is the project of communication philosophy set in the perspective of transcendental pragmatics (TP),[2] in the basic shape constructed by Karl-Otto Apel[3] (1973) almost half a century ago, which still has the possibility of developing its philosophical threads in relation to a whole range of issues, both theoretical and practical in nature.[4] Among these issues is the aggression observed in the communication space, which turns out to be an issue of extraordinary importance for transcendental-pragmatic philosophical reflection.

It is not easy to make a concise, brief reconstruction of the transcendental-pragmatic project of communication philosophy. The scale of the difficulty of such a measure is determined not only by the degree of complication of this concept but also by the fact that its complete shape consists of resolutions that were directly and literally proposed by the creators of transcendental pragmatics, resolutions closely related to the proposed ones or resolutions that were a significant inspiration for them, and finally resolutions that seem to be their possible (important and rich) consequences. A detailed analysis of the genesis of the individual elements that constitute this project must be abandoned at this point. This will significantly reduce the value of the reconstruction but will allow for completing the presentation of the transcendental-pragmatic project of communication philosophy in several crucial points, both essential and relevant, especially due to the problem of communicative aggression. Here are the most important of these points:

1 The overriding theoretical procedure undertaken by TP is the **transformation of Kantian's transcendentalism** (Apel 1973) as a philosophical theory, which, in the history of European philosophy, is unparalleled in terms of the radicalism with which it undertook the work of the critical penetration of cognitive powers in search of the indestructible foundations of knowledge. By positioning itself in the Kantian perspective, TP was able to approach a philosophical problem of the greatest gravity, a philosophical question par excellence, that is, the question of knowledge, including its conditions, meaningfulness and importance, and the possibility of its definitive justification. This is the essential theoretical field of TP (Apel 1978; Kuhlmann 1988).

2 Although philosophical questions and problems are definitely of the Kantian provenance in TP, both (a) the ways of conceptualizing knowledge itself and its subject and (b) the procedures by which knowledge becomes justified are clearly distinct in this field of inquiry. In other words, the approach to each of these issues is shaped in TP by referring to **communicative *a priori*** and the discursive[5] nature of communicative rationality (Apel 1973, 1986; Kuhlmann 1985b). Kantian's transcendentalism, despite its groundbreaking nature, shared a classical error with traditional concepts: namely, it omitted linguistic communication practices, which was, in fact, a simple consequence of the traditional way of conceptualizing language, that is, a theoretical approach to it that abstracts from its pragmatic and performative aspect. It is this (serious and severe in terms of consequences) theoretical deficiency, defined as *abstractive fallacy*, that is eliminated in the process of

the transcendental-pragmatic transformation of Kantianism. Nonetheless, it is extremely important that the communicative dimension does not appear here as a complement or addition to the construction of knowledge, but it is in this dimension that fundamental knowledge-creating potential is recognized (which TP owes mainly to Pierce and Wittgenstein). Knowledge is not only embedded in communication processes but also derives its most important characteristics from the structures of communication acts and relations, and, most of all, due to them, it is possible to definitively justify it. Placing communication cooperation in the center of knowledge-creating processes consequently leads to a reshaping of the main problem area within epistemological as well as ontological and ethical reflection, and therefore naturally also of other areas covered by philosophical consideration.

3   The indication of the primary and constitutive nature of communication processes in relation to knowledge, social existence, and the ethical foundations of the human world closely corresponds to the emphasis on communicative competence as decisive for the essential characteristics of humans. In terms of communication philosophy, communicative competence can no longer be perceived as just one of many abilities we are provided with, even if placed among the abilities of the highest importance. Contrary to many theories, both historical and contemporary, communicative competence should definitely be considered an exceptional, original, and specific human ability, indeed, an essential characteristic of humans. The human being is, above all, a communicating being—*homo communicativus*.

This observation, extremely important, accurate, and rich in theoretical consequences, does not mean that the concept of humans as "communicatively modeled" should be placed in the center of philosophical research on communication and that the tools for analyzing the situation and communication processes should be derived from it. Nor does it mean that the whole structure of communication philosophy should be based on the philosophy of man as *homo communicativus*. Rather, this fundamental level, which marks the theoretical starting point for the transcendental-pragmatic theory, is, in line with the spirit of Kantianism, the analysis of knowledge-creating processes. And these processes, which Kantianism did make visible, are embedded in **linguistic communication practices** (Apel 1973).

4   Thus, it is the linguistic communication practices that determine the basic level of transcendental-pragmatic analyses, and these determine the way of problematizing all important philosophical issues. The most important findings of these analyses include the recognition that the dual, performative-propositional structure of linguistic acts determines the pragmatic and performative nature of communication processes in general, which means that what we define as a communication act is, in fact, always communication cooperation, that is, it is communicative coaction mediated by a linguistic symbol.[6]

   Indubitably, the discoveries of John Austin, and later also of John Searle, who in their analyses of language managed to shift the theoretical attention from the content of a linguistic utterance to its illocutionary force, and from its meaning to its illocutionary force, were extremely important (in fact, revolutionary and groundbreaking). However, to fully understand the phenomena of communication, it is absolutely necessary to highlight and derive consequences from the fact that communication actions are always **shared and reciprocal activities**. Therefore, it is decisive to focus attention on those characteristics that are condensed in this "co-." This prefix fundamentally changes the meaning of all the categories it accompanies, which is especially important in the case of the meanings behind the terms "co-action," "co-operation," "co-intentionality," and "co-responsibility."

5   Another very important circumstance is related to the fact that in the area of communication (i.e., communication mediated by linguistic symbols), we tackle activities with special properties that definitely stand out from all other human activities. What distinguishes them is their ability to be **self-relevant**. At a fundamental level, self-relevance, like cooperation, is a trait coupled with the dual performative and propositional nature of the linguistic act (Kuhlmann 1981). It means the possibility of *explicitly* formulating those contents that (as the contents accompanying the thematized, propositional part of the linguistic act) are *implicitly* included in the performative layer of this act. The ability to make this kind of transformation pertains to the essence of communication competence.

6   This *explicitly* unspoken content, as accompanying knowledge—always and forever present in the act of communication—is a set of **obligations, duties, claims, and presuppositions**,[7] which affect its fulfillment, and whose presence determines the possibility of

communication cooperation. They, in turn, are accompanied by—also *implicitly* included—arguments that problematize and establish them, which indicate the conditions that determine whether and when these obligations are eligible and the linguistic act is successful. To put it simply, they serve to argue for and against the application and justification of obligations, duties, claims, and presuppositions introduced by the linguistic act into the performative layer. Their inalienable presence in the linguistic act and the possibility of expressing them *explicitly* make it an **argumentative act** (Kuhlmann 1981; Apel 1996). Nevertheless, argumentation of this act does not end there, since the arguments under consideration, and this is a key point, are also accompanied by a set of *implicitly* introduced obligations, which may also need to be established, and this is again possible only through argumentation. At each level of the argumentation procedure, as the only tool for problematizing and establishing our arguments, the "reference" is a specific set of obligations, duties, claims, and presuppositions, and this set is also always problematized through the argumentation procedure. Thus, at every level, the argumentative situation is essentially uncircumventable, which, on the basis of TP, is precisely proved by the so-called close reflection[8] and allows us to speak of the argumentative nature of human rationality.

7. It is important, however, that TP does not equate argumentation with the "formal and logically objectifiable structure of explanation" related to the content conveyed in the propositional layer but rather distinguishes it as a procedure related only to the sphere of obligations (claims, duties, and presuppositions) and oriented, generally, toward their justification. Moreover, demonstrating that the argumentative situation understood in this way is uncircumventable, that it is an inalienable element of all the processes that comprise linguistic communication practices, TP recognizes that—to put it in the categories proposed by Ludwig Wittgenstein—the argumentative game is not one of many possible language games (communication) but is a game of a special status, a game not only constitutive for human rationality but also a **transcendental game**, one that determines the *a priori* conditions for the possibility of every other game and thus the conditions for the possibility of communication in general (Apel 1986). Argumentation understood in this way is referred to in TP as discursive argumentation, simply called discourse.[9] The discursive nature of communication, or its

**discursiveness**, is a fundamental (though deeply hidden) characteristic of communication processes, the violation of which always threatens with their destruction or severe mutilation.

8. A particular subtlety in the method of implementing discursiveness is related to the fact that the condition for the possibility of the communication act is not a specific circumstance, a documented fact, or a reliable diagnosis but just a claim or obligation, that is, an intentionally contributed interest. And being intentionally contributed interest, it has a **counterfactual** status (Habermas 1981) in that it is essentially aimed at perfect fulfillment, which is never actually achieved. In its content, it anticipates its ideal realization, but it is only anticipation. Anticipating a **definitive consensus** on claims, that is, a perfect agreement on them, is a situation in which the claims are no longer problematized (Apel 1996).

The definitive consensus is not, therefore, the state of knowledge, but it constitutes a specific normative structure that determines the validity status of knowledge. The purpose to which it is subordinated is to indicate the process of consensual agreement as the only valid way in which procedures legitimizing the validity of knowledge can be implemented and in which specific criteria for its validity can be obtained.

This anticipated condition of the definitive consensus is, in fact, a synonym of the **ideal** (unlimited) **communication community**[10] as a regulating idea constructed in the inalienable tension with the real community and, in this tension, defining the horizon of real communication practices.[11]

9. The normative and counterfactual status of both the ideal communication community and the principles of the perfect consensus (and with it, the claims, obligations, and duties themselves) remains the carrier of the fundamental regulations indispensable for the functioning of the real communication community. The **normativity and counterfactual** nature of the idea of the definitive consensus and the ideal communication community, enigmatic and seemingly "cumbersome" in practical application, are immanently inscribed in the structure of the communication relation, which forces constant efforts to realize them, and consequently makes it necessary to maintain the conditions for the possibility of making them real. In this pursuit of the fulfillment of claims and duties, with the intention of reaching the definitive consensus in the tension between the ideal and real communication community, lies the essence

of human rationality. This striving manifests in every, even the simplest, communication act, determining the possibility of the communication relation in general, that is, the possibility of every communication event and process. The presence of this striving and its essential content are not a question of political beliefs, ideological declarations, or religious inclinations. And although each of these dimensions can find—and indeed does—a more or less unambiguous expression in the way we thematize these efforts, they are deeply (and authoritatively) motivated by the very structure of the communication relation. Contrary to our quite natural feeling that we, as subjects of the communication relation, impose the norms, claims, and duties that determine it, we must accept that their rigor results directly from the formal requirements of communication cooperation. It is not us who set these requirements!

What, unfortunately, is within our capabilities is the possibility of the destruction of these requirements; the disturbance of their subtle game with reality; and, finally, their fully effective annihilation. In fact, we face this "possibility" due to the aggression that accompanies the communication processes taking place in the megamedia space.

This is not only due to the fact that aggressive communication behaviors undermine claims, breach obligations, or do not fulfill duties, which—as accompanying knowledge (*knowhow*)—are introduced in the performative layer of each communication act. For example, these aggressive behaviors breach the obligation to recognize the co-partnership of other communication participants, to respect their independence in choices and argumentative decisions, to treat them subjectively, and to consider them as entities capable of truth and rational argumentation.

By all means, there is no doubt that aggression manifested in such a way, like all the other negative phenomena observed in the megamedia space,[12] is extremely dangerous in each of the three specified aspects, that is, security, freedom, and dignity, in all their dimensions and on every scale. In fact, media aggression completely annihilates these aspects; it completely deprives the participants of communication of their security and dignity, and completely enslaves them in terms of their choices. It is equally obvious that these phenomena of megamedia aggression constitute a huge problem today, and in view of their scale and the specific nature of the megamedia space within which they appear, they oblige us to take extraordinary care and decisive counteraction. However, from the point of view of the specificity of discursiveness, the presence of the phenomena of megamedia aggression is basically "natural." After all, claims and obligations are of a counterfactual nature, and, as such, they are anticipations of their ideal fulfillment and are never fulfilled in the real communication community. Invariably constituting the content of aspirations and imperative orders, these claims and obligations still remain an extremely urgent task, and not only on the basis of megamedia communication.

It is precisely on this basis that we are facing a problem of the most serious nature, with a perplexity that cannot be accepted from a practical or theoretical point of view. The main danger connected with aggression in the megamedia space is that it destroys and prevents discourse. It obstructs the pursuit of the consensus, prevents the maintenance of the necessary reference to the ideal communication community, and leads to breaking the subtle line of tension between an ideal and a real community. All this is due to the fact that its blade is actually aimed at cooperation.

Meanwhile, communicative activity is, by nature, a shared, reciprocal activity—it is always cooperation.[13] The fact that it is co-intentionally shaped collaboration is also constitutive for it. Cooperation does not amount to the fact that the content of the communication act must be addressed to a partner or a group of partners (to the "other"), that the message is passed between the sender and the receiver, or that an agreement as to the communicated content is achieved through a shared interpretative effort.[14] Cooperation in communication is much more: it is sharing common communication intentions, their co-creation, and the shared and reciprocal shaping of the conditions for the anticipated consensus as well as the joint guidelines of its scope (thus, the simultaneous determination of the outlines of the ideal communication community); the joint building of the space for discursiveness; and, finally, the constructive supervising of the relation "real–ideal communication community."

In all these scopes, indisputably constitutive for the processes of communication and, at the same time, absolutely requiring communication cooperation, the violation of cooperation always brings the same result: it prevents the possibility of discourse to a greater or lesser extent. And, in view of the extraordinary rank of discursiveness (both in reference to the individual acts of communication and to human rationality in general), it even leads to the ditching of human rationality,[15] which is always associated with the threat of annihilation of the communication community or at least its severe mutilation.

Aggression is the source of the most serious violations and the strongest threat to cooperation in the communication space (as a guarantee of the possibility of discourse and thus of human rationality). In each of its forms, as physical aggression (not included here but obviously not ignored), as communicative aggression in general, or specifically as aggression observed in the megamedia space, it always has a destructive effect on the possibility of cooperation. It always, to a greater or lesser extent, destroys the structures that are the carriers of cooperation, destroys the relations (not only communication) within which and due to which cooperation has a chance to develop and survive.

Undoubtedly, the strength and "effectiveness" of this destructiveness vary, as does the resistance to it. The mechanisms of a psychological nature are not considered here, although they definitely require separate, meticulous attention and may await effective therapeutic support. However, the most powerful "shock wave" of aggression exists in the purely formal structures at the heart of the communication relation, to which no therapeutic support can be granted. Broken and destroyed mechanisms just do not work. There are no measures (or half measures) to restore their functionality. This situation is comparable to the processes of environmental devastation. All we can do is stop our actions against it, as the clock is still ticking, until it is not too late. Crossing a specific line in terms of the destruction of certain fundamental mechanisms of the functioning of the natural environment no longer offers a chance to reverse the situation. The social environment is exposed to exactly the same scenario, which is still difficult for us to see and accept. The history of the greatest social disasters clearly confirms this. Unnoticed in time, they are unstoppable.

However, to recognize the symptoms, to catch and reveal the "harbingers" of a disaster, is a special mission that is exposed to enormous difficulties not only at the level of substantive analyses but also due to multiple non-substantive factors (political, economic, ideological, psychological, and many others).

For the transcendental-pragmatic communication philosophy, which obviously undertakes such a mission, the most important and unanswered questions (disregarding, certainly, non-substantive factors) concern the extent to which the new media reality, characterized as megamedia, intensifies the destructive power of aggression. What is the reason for this special danger that lies behind the aggression observed in the megamedia space? Is it really bigger than what the media world has exposed us to so far?

The answer to these questions is an unequivocal "yes"; the magnitude of megamedia aggression is unparalleled and brings the highest, unprecedented threat to the world of interpersonal communication! What is the reason for the radicalism of this answer? What is the basis of it? Primarily, it results from the recognition that communicative aggression **destroys the deep structures of the communication relation**, which are the conditions for the possibility of cooperation that is realized within this relation. Furthermore, this radicalism has its source in the perception that processes that were **real communication** (authentic communication and thus assuming all its constitutive aspects) became possible only in the megamedia space and could not take place in the field of mass media communication. There is also a third important circumstance, which is that communication processes that take place in the megamedia space are characterized by an **unprecedented scale**: an unprecedented range, availability, frequency, multiplication, and many other characteristics, which cause each phenomenon observed to have a completely new impact, including aggression. Finally, the image of the whole is complemented by what is already common (and, until recently, sounded futuristic): our interpersonal communication has already **transferred**, to a large extent, to the megamedia space (and the question is—rather sentimental and rhetorical—whether it will come back sometime).

However, while maintaining the due seriousness in this matter, it must also be clearly indicated that each of these four processes is irreversible. Each has its own "ironclad logic" that, once activated, cannot be stopped. By conditioning and complementing each other, these processes create a "composition" that determines the answer to the formulated questions and determines the final diagnosis, which is binding for TP. In the shortest formulation, the diagnosis is as follows: aggression observed in the megamedia space constitutes a threat of the highest importance to the foundations of communication, which is the threat of destroying the basic social bond and thus of annihilating the communication community.

## Notes

1 It should be noted that in the literature on the subject, such a terminological distinction is not common (both concepts are called the "philosophy of communication").

2 The abbreviation "TP" is used wherever it is possible to replace the term "transcendental pragmatics" with it (although some contexts require the use of the full term).
3 The leading advocates and followers, and with regard to certain important theoretical issues, also co-creators of the transcendental-pragmatic concept, are Wolfgang Kuhlmann (1981, 1985b) and Dietrich Böhler (1985, 1994).
4 From the point of view of my own research interests, I found the possibility of using transcendental-pragmatic tools for justifying philosophical criticism as well as exposing the specificity of the so-called "discursive attitude," to which I devoted a book entitled *Criticism and Discourse [Krytyka i dyskurs]* (Sierocka 2003). Both in that book and in my articles, I have succeeded in demonstrating the usefulness of these tools in relation to many other important and difficult philosophical problems.
5 The term "discursiveness" acquires a special meaning in the context of TP, which is explained further in this chapter.
6 The attempt at a full definition of communication is presented in Chapter 2.
7 The content related to claims, obligations, duties, and presuppositions included in communication processes is further discussed in Chapter 6. Here, just to mention, and which is already commonly known, the approach to these issues—originally suggested by John Searle (in the form of conditions for the effectiveness of acts speech (Searle 1975)), and then developed by Jürgen Habermas (1981) on the basis of universal pragmatics, and finally (with some exceptions) adapted by Karl-Otto Apel (1973, 1996) in transcendental pragmatics—mainly accentuates four groups of validity claims, that is, claims to (1) intersubjectively shared sense, (2) truthfulness, (3) truth, and (4) normative rightness.
8 Strict reflection is a non-educational way of carrying out the justifying procedure, on which the entire theoretical construction of TP is supported and which (as it may be said) is its way of restoring transcendentalism and freeing it from methodical solipsism, which, according to the diagnosis already present by Peirce, is on Kantianism. The details of this procedure are discussed in Chapter 6.
9 The legitimacy of this term can be confirmed by the fact (however, it is a coincidence) that the etymological term "discourse" indicates "running back and forth," and this is exactly what we are dealing with here: the transition from obligations to arguments, from arguments to obligations, without the possibility of going beyond this argumentative circle. Its exceeding this means falling into a performative self-contradiction, and this means abandoning communicative rationality.
10 The general idea of the unlimited communication community is derived through transcendental pragmatics from the idea formulated by Charles Peirce, in the context of the problem of truth, in the *Indefinite Community of Investigators* (Apel 1973).
11 It is very important and rich in consequences that the Kantian transcendental unity of apperception, which is Kant's "peak" of the transcendental deduction of principles, is replaced by the postulate of the definitive consensus of the unlimited communication community in the transcendental-pragmatic project.

12 Listed in Chapter 3.
13 See Chapter 2 as well as Chapter 5.
14 A similar understanding of communicative "co-engagement" can be found, for example, in the works of the founders of the philosophy of dialogue (Buber 2008), in the concept of Roman Jakobson (1960), and in the hermeneutics of Hans-Georg Gadamer (1960).
15 This issue is presented more elaborately in Chapter 6.

# 5 Mutualism, Co-Intentionality, Trust

The diagnoses that TP relates to the phenomena of megamedia aggression are embedded in the communication philosophy project underlying them and obtained due to philosophical communication theory tools.[1] At the same time, these diagnoses often find support and very important inspiration in many external philosophical concepts, including those that, in terms of their program, break away from the idea of transcendentalism or base their constructions on other theoretical "levels." This most fundamental level, determined by the apriorism of transcendental pragmatics, allows for an interesting and conclusive way to build new levels over it, on which it is possible—in a theoretical dialogue with the resolutions external to TP—to conceptualize many important philosophical issues. A good example here is the concept of truth, on the basis of which TP reconciles, in an original and convincing way, four different philosophical approaches, namely correspondence, consensual, fallibilistic, and transcendental. With regard to communication issues, a long-standing dispute (and, at the same time, cooperation) between transcendental pragmatics and the universal pragmatics of Jürgen Habermas has become paradigmatic—very fruitful, though invariably polemic. This ability of TP for conclusive dialogue with different philosophical options is a very valuable trait.

Equally important is its openness to research and non-philosophical theories. In terms of communication issues, TP has close relations with many different disciplines. In this group, apart from linguistics and the philological sciences, are psychology (in its various subdisciplines), cultural sciences, comparative anthropology, sociology, cultural anthropology, neurobiology, media studies, political science, and management theory. These quite extensive, as for philosophy, connections with the empirical disciplines—their dispersion and wide range—are not only the result of the substantive "embedding" of TP in the subject of communication but, most of all, the consequences of its special modeling, which has given it the status of "communication philosophy." This means that it is a specific way of philosophical thinking, a specific research method, and a specific type of approach to the problematized issues: namely, those that are invariably based on the idea of communicative *a priori* and which consistently apply the communication theory tools to each philosophical issue. These circumstances determine that any type of research is of the utmost importance for the TP project, which, to some extent, brings an understanding of communication phenomena closer, allows for a proper assessment of their rank, and, above all, strengthens TP in its theoretical efforts to highlight the most important threats and duties resulting from them, which weigh heavily on society as the real communication community. Due to this strengthening, it is easier to explain the manifestations of aggression in the megamedia space.

In this respect, the most valuable inspirations come from those non-philosophical concepts which, when faced with the question about the fundamental determinants of the human condition, that is, the determinants of our cultural and social life, reveal (and document with their research) the importance of human **collaboration** in all these dimensions. And, because it is collaboration, in the form of communication cooperation, that suffers the most serious mutilation from aggressive megamedia behaviors, revealing the mechanisms that determine collaboration, and thoroughly understanding its meaning, is the starting point for diagnosing the destructive force of these behaviors and, at the same time, a source of valuable indications as to the need for their absolute elimination. In other words, to understand collaboration is to grasp the most important premises imposing the compulsion of absolute opposition to megamedia aggression.

However, the question of collaboration is one in which the answer is very complicated and still open, and, even more importantly, it is a question that in the long history of reflection on the human world has moved to the "front line of scientific research" with great difficulty. Indeed, it was hardly perceived as a serious theoretical issue, and thus it had no chance to become the key to resolutions of a fundamental nature for a long time. The situation only changed due to transformations of the intellectual paradigm in the social sciences and humanities, which took place at the beginning of the 20th century, along with the pragmatic turn and associated ennoblement of the "anthropological perspective" (which we owe to the Polish anthropologist Bronisław Malinowski[2] (Malinowski 1923; Sierocka 2003).

The breakthrough nature of these transformations was that they opened the possibility of conceptualizing particular spheres of cultural reality as various **forms of social practice** and, on the other side of the coin, made it possible to understand that it is at the level of social practices (such as linguistic communication practices) that the essential determinants of this reality should be sought.

Incidentally, the additional and very important "profit" from these transformations was the construction of original critical tools, which (in the spirit of Kant's transcendental dialectic)[3] serve to reveal loops, hypostases, and appearances in which rationality, closed in the so-called "theoretical attitude" and deprived of the possibility of transcending it toward the "discursive attitude,"[4] involves us in an inappreciable way. (As to see rationality locked in the "theoretical attitude" is to see to what extent its fundamental features are determined by the specificity of social practices that are at its foundation).

Therefore, when all these theoretical circumstances gradually redirected the attention of researchers to the sphere of activities and actions that comprise the space of culturally shaped social practices, the need for an understanding of the mechanisms that determine the possibility of these practices arose quite naturally. The search for resolutions in this respect has obviously led to many different opinions. However, what is important is the fact that among them, there were some on the basis of which a kind of turn took place, which was unquestionably Kant's Copernican revolution in philosophy. Its essence, similar to Kant's, came down to reversing the arrow direction illustrating the fundamental relation, in this case the relation: "**individual–collective**."

Psychologists, anthropologists, philosophers, sociologists, and even neuroscientists frequently have proposed resolutions that, in a more or less open and conscious way, undermine the traditional scheme, according to which the sum of particular competences, particular acts, and individual characteristics is ultimately to constitute the phenomenon of collectivism, that is, the possibility of sharing tasks and undertaking common group ventures, and, thus, the implementation of culturally shaped social practices. More and more often, these studies suggest that this traditional pattern is, in fact, an obstacle to understanding and explaining the most important phenomena of the social world. "Particular–common," "individual–collective," and "single–group" are therefore distinctions that, first, science begins to perceive as key, and thus as those by means of which all the most important issues concerning humans and their world should be problematized, and for which, second, the perception of relations that occur within them must be unconditionally revised, and, therefore, simply put, the primacy and superiority of what is of a collective, common, and group nature should be noticed and emphasized.

This superiority itself can be understood in various ways, as different sciences have different explanatory possibilities in this regard. It can be conceptualized differently on the basis of psychology, sociology, neurobiology, anthropology, philosophy, and so on, and this difference between the possible approaches seems very beneficial and promising. Different sciences and individual theorists are trying to find answers to the (most difficult here) questions in different ways, that is, questions about the detailed determinants shaping these distinctions (Gouldner 1960; Mauss 1966; Grice 1975; Searle 1995; Dunbar 2007; Tomasello 2009; Baron-Cohen 2011; Hill 2012). Most researchers are aware that numerous subtleties cannot be satisfactorily explained here, but an increasing number of studies show that it is the phenomenon of collective cooperation that is the key to understanding all social reality, regardless of the perspective from which such research is undertaken. Regardless of whether they are related to, for example, the concept of the collective human nature, the theory of the social brain, collective intentionality, empathy, the paradigmatic principle of reciprocity or communication cooperation, each of these approaches in a valuable way brings us closer to recognizing the real character of these distinctions, to an understanding of the complex interrelations between what is individual and particular and what is collective and common.

It is not known how long the way to complete success is here. Nonetheless, it is certainly known that this is the only way that gives a chance to understand our social condition, especially in the face of all the uncertainties that the current shape of the social world brings, including its megamedia character.

The fact that this is the only way has been confirmed by many recent research projects, but from the perspective of the diagnoses that can be formulated by transcendental pragmatics, it definitely draws the strongest support and the deepest theoretical suggestions from the concept developed by Michael Tomasello (1999, 2009).[5]

First, this is because the original research and equally original theoretical resolutions proposed by Tomasello form an extremely coherent and logical structure, allowing for the conceptualization of a full range of phenomena that can be considered by psychology, anthropology, philosophy, sociology, history, and a few other empirical disciplines. This naturally determines the extraordinary conclusiveness of this concept, especially with regard to the problem of the "particular–collective" distinction.

Second, and which is even more important from the TP perspective, the directions of interpretation followed by Tomasello are exactly the "nerve" of the philosophical tradition that determined the possibility of constituting "communication philosophy" as a specific form of today's philosophical theory. We are talking here, most importantly, about the direction marked by the concept of a "late thought" of Wittgenstein, which focused on the new approach to the question of meaning (interestingly anticipated in the work of Bronisław Malinowski (1923)). This is the line that is culminated by Tomasello's concept in a particularly valuable way. At the same time, Tomasello's analyses, consistently carried out in the spirit of Wittgenstein, are a testimony to an interesting and valuable translation of Wittgenstein's philosophy into issues that go far beyond the traditional scope of philosophical reflection and, at the same time, are very important to it.

Additionally, all theoretical threads, in a more or less obvious way, are included in Tomasello's reflection on the complexity of the "individual–collective" relation. From the perspective of this distinction, issues related to human cognitive abilities, the mechanisms of cultural evolution, and the methods of the establishment and functioning of social institutions and normative systems are problematized. Undoubtedly, it is this distinction, together with the answer to the question of what specific relations connect both of its parts, that must be considered superior and thus ordering all the other historically dominant lines of theoretical tensions. Moreover, it should define the overriding problem area of all sciences that ask in any way about humans and their world.

Finally, and most importantly, the dimension of what is supraindividual, collective, and common is perceived in this concept in a special way: always as the space for common action, participation in activities, sharing goals and intentions, reciprocity in shaping the norms of behavior, and the common construction of social institutions. All these shared activities comprise the phenomenon of communication cooperation and are simultaneously conditioned by it. Communication cooperation is expressed in them, is realized by means of them, and simultaneously shapes them. These are very complex relations and dependencies that are definitely not easy to reconstruct, and by devoting most of his research to them, Tomasello allows us to see in collaboration (always communicative by nature) the fundamental level of shaping social reality, the source of unique human culture, and even a specific "incubator" of being human.

All these circumstances mean that Tomasello's concept (the hypotheses he formulates and the research and analyses he conducts) should be assessed as currently the most important scientific partner for communication philosophy. It is a partner which, in the group of non-philosophical disciplines (although, as I suggested, in a deeply philosophical, Wittgensteinian tone), most strongly and consistently emphasizes the importance of communication cooperation, and, based on its research, builds argumentative structures that strengthen the thesis about communicative *a priori*, which is fundamental to this philosophy in a particularly valuable way. But, most of all, it is the partner which, exactly in the collaborative nature of communication, allows for noticing its most important feature and, grandly speaking, allows for the understanding that collaboration is the key to the human world.

At the same time, research on collaboration opened another important problem area in relation to Tomasello's concept, which is the question about the real source of the "natural human readiness to cooperate" observed on the basis of this research and, even more precisely, the question of whether a person acquires this readiness through socialization or owes it to inborn altruism (as a tendency to be helpful, to be instructive, or to be generous (Warneken 2009)). Turning these issues into original research experiments (both in the field of primatology and developmental psychology) has brought many very interesting findings, among which the strongest implications should be attributed to a very important suggestion formulated on the basis of them, which, to put it briefly, shifts the weight of the entire problem from altruism to mutuality. Admittedly, this suggestion has a very laconic wording in Tomasello's research; however, it evokes associations with issues already considered to some extent on the basis of the social sciences and philosophy. In the approach proposed by Tomasello, it is important to establish that humans share their altruistic inclinations with their closest relatives from the primate order and that, therefore, it is not altruism that determines the specificity of human behavior, and it is not altruism to which human culture owes its uniqueness. The framework in which the altruistic attitude of humanity is revealed is determined by **mutualism,** and it is mutualism that plays the most important role in modeling human activities. If altruism could be reduced to the formula "I act for your benefit," then mutualism can be ascribed the formula "we act together for the common benefit." Therefore, mutualism, as Tomasello puts it, "is that we all benefit from our cooperation, but only when we work together." We benefit from the fact that we engage in collaboration.

Nevertheless, with some irony, it can be said that the greatest benefits, those on an exorbitant scale, are experienced primarily by culture, which is the real beneficiary here. The birth of mutuality is, in fact, the birth of communication relations. After all, the communication relation is precisely the unique space in which it becomes possible to constitute and reveal these common benefits (as common goals and shared intentions) and to initiate common activities (as collaboration based on states of common attention). Along with all this, as Tomasello (1999) shows, the conditions for cumulative cultural evolution are born. Thus, human culture is born and the human world is created.

The mutualistic context of human communication, and therefore the essentially normative[6] and imperatively binding subtext of the formula "we act together for common benefit," is the fundamental determinant of communication cooperation. Therefore, this mutualistic context is also the primary aspect of our communicative competence, the main determinant of its unique character (and, at the same time, the determinant allowing for the suggestion that those forms of communicative contact that have not been established within a relation shaped in a mutualistic way are, at best, manifestations of proto-communication but not proper communication).[7] Somewhat paradoxically, it should be said that the elementary traits of individual communication competences definitely go beyond individual abilities, intentions, or motivations. Using the beautiful phrase by Hanse-Georg Gadamer, "not you, not me – and yet we," it can be summed up like this: I get involved in the communication relation, you get involved in it, but it really only takes place provided that it transforms us into "we." It is only in this "we" that the set of activities that constitute the act of communication cooperation takes place. We become and remain the subjects of communication only as "we." Therefore, the destruction of "we," the destruction of its determinants (predominantly including claims for the consensus), is the destruction of the entire communicative situation. It is the abolition of the conditions of the possibility of the communication relation and thus the possibility of the real communication community. Only the strength of mutualistic ties protects against such consequences. This is where its fundamental role lies and, hence, its extraordinary importance.

In fact, the problem of mutualism has never appeared before in the humanities or the social sciences (apart from the political context, but here there was simply a justified coincidence of terms). In view of the importance of the perspective that mutualism provides, this absence is very surprising. Perhaps the ultimate reason for this is precisely the fact that this problem simply could not arise until these sciences ennobled the sphere of communication and, most of all, until it was possible to problematize this sphere through the prism of the double structure of communication acts and thus through the prism of its illocutionary force, and, finally, collaboration.

Despite the fact that no one spoke directly about mutualism, the intuitions of many theorists were, in some way, directed toward it— especially the intuition of anthropologists (whether defined as social or cultural ones). This is most easily captured in their research on phenomena, behaviors, and attitudes related to the principle (or rule) of reciprocity (Malinowski 1922, 1926; Gouldner 1960; Sahlins 1965; Mauss 1966; Levi-Strauss 1969). These researchers—whether it was in a detailed reconstruction of the functioning of the mechanisms of reciprocity in indigenous communities or constructing a typology of these phenomena and enclosing them with theoretical explanations—obviously put the strongest emphasis on the culturally legitimized commitment to repay, that is, the obligation to reciprocate earlier gestures; politeness; and, above all, gifts according to the principle of *do ut des:* "I give, so that you may give." However, the explanations and descriptions of the functioning of this principle, as presented by these researchers, allow us to notice that, in fact, being a cultural universal, it owes its versatility to the skill that is fundamental to the communication relation and the tendency of its participants to share obligations and satisfy reciprocal claims. Reciprocity as a principle is constituted and "practiced and exercised" in the most basic communicative situations and is absolutely required in these situations. It is on the basis of communication cooperation that reciprocity primarily proves its indispensability. Therefore, regardless of how to evaluate relatively long disputes (not only of anthropologists) over the genesis, scope, and social significance of the principle of reciprocity, it must not be missed that its original matrix is integrated into the structure of the act of communication cooperation shaped in a mutualistic way, and that this is what explains the omnipresence of this principle, which is confirmed on the basis of psychology, economics, sociology, anthropology, management theory, and several other disciplines, penetrating quite distant fields of the human life. The other side of this coin is, and should be, the recognition and understanding of the extent to which reciprocity—in this fundamental sense, as (conditioning the possibility of cooperation) reciprocal respect and fulfillment of claims and obligations and maintaining reciprocally beneficial relations—requires absolute protection, "care," and indeed cultivation.

The reciprocity inherent in the mutualistic structure of the act of communication cooperation is also manifested at a different level; namely, it is related to the intentions and goals that direct these communication acts, and, therefore, generally, to the intentionality that accompanies them. These references open the way to perhaps the most powerful set of factors that determine our communication practices. Also, the discovery of how intentionality forms communication interactions in a specific way is another great contribution of Tomasello's research and concept, and, at the same time, a very important trace for philosophy—in this case, not only for communication philosophy.

Linking the communication processes with intentionality is not a rare procedure. Many research trends, especially those of pragmatic provenance, even assume that, as Sperber and Wilson (2012, p. 261) wrote, "the essential feature of most communication between people, both verbal and non-verbal, is the expression and recognition of intentions." However, Tomasello's concept, despite the fact that it tends to treat intentionality as a specific and distinctive feature, does not follow this attitude. This difference results from the fact that this concept takes a significant theoretical turn, in principle comparable to that experienced by philosophy, which is abandoning the subjectivist perspective in favor of the intersubjective approach, or crossing the mentalist paradigm in favor of the linguistic-communicative perspective. Although these transitions seem to be purely categorical transformations, in fact, they have brought theoretical thought to a whole new level, liberating it from previously insurmountable disabilities and aporias. Tomasello's concept has exactly the same potential. This is the result of two theoretical steps that take place there, which are interconnected yet separate. Both, by all means, are about intentionality.

First of all, what Tomasello sees as the key to our communication cooperation is not simply intentionality but rather co-intentionality, which is understood as the ability, inclination, and motivation to share intentions, to participate in the scene of joint attention and in states of common attention, to build common goals jointly, to shape intentions collaboratively and reciprocally, and to transform them together (and create common goals and intentions).

Co-intentionality, apart from the motivation for engaging in common ventures, determines pragmatic competence and therefore determines the possibility of every communication act and relation. On the other hand, the coordinating of common intentions and actions, and the joint and reciprocal coordination of roles, requires cooperation and therefore the ability to communicate. Co-intentionality, as Tomasello shows, is therefore immanently linked with communication cooperation. This discovery does not invalidate the indications for intentionality as the ability to express and recognize intentions. Nonetheless, it is not this skill that "carries" the burden of real communication and that determines the uniqueness of the collaborative relation that arises between people. We owe this to co-intentionality.

Second, Tomasello's research sensitizes us to the special status of co-intentionality. Namely, it allows us to see that co-intentionality is not simply a derivative of the intentionality characteristic of individuals, that is, not the creation of particular intentions. What Tomasello discovered in his research (and what John Searle suggested as collective intentionality in a rather abstract approach) is an ability that is available, admittedly, only to intentional beings, but in no way is reducible to the sum of particular intentions. This ability is what "embeds" particular activities and intentions in the social, culture-forming processes. It "engages" particular intentions in collective action and determines particular behaviors and intentions, but it does not exist outside of them. Once again, it must be said, in parallel to the quoted phrase by Gadamer, that the level at which the main game takes place here is "we," not "you" and "me." This, then, is we-intentionality.

We-intentionality, like the mutualistic nature of the communication relation, is a dimension that is extremely difficult to conceptualize, and yet it is revealed in Tomasello's research in a very inspiring and credible way. The access to this dimension was, to some extent, prepared in 20th-century philosophy and sociology, especially in those theories in which (each in a different way but with equal theoretical commitment) attempts were made to move reflection beyond the classic distinctions of the following type: "subjective–objective," "subject–object," and "special–general"— distinctions not so difficult to conceptualize but, as we know today, much less credible (e.g., Mead 1934; Gadamer 1960; Adorno 1966; Searle 1969; Wittgenstein 1977; Simmel, 1992). The theory built by

Tomasello, the individual resolutions he proposes, and even his individual suggestions, seem to fit precisely into the trend of these theoretical efforts. This, it seems, gives particular insight into the approach of this concept to such complicated problem complexes as those determined by mutualism and intentionality. At the same time, it should be remembered that theoretical reflection on these issues is especially important because they conceal important normative potential, and they indirectly define the content of strict obligations and imply an absolute requirement to meet them. All this becomes particularly valuable in the context of threats that the sphere of communication cooperation is facing from media aggression (and, above all, from megamedia aggression).

Another aspect of the equal importance of mutualism and intentionality, and of a similar scale of difficulty that arises when trying to conceptualize it in the context of communication cooperation, is **trust**. Trust is a category that has been faced by thinkers in social philosophy for over three centuries (Hobbes 1651; Locke 1689), and gradually they were joined by numerous theorists from the fields of economics, political science, sociology, psychology, and management theory (Erikson 1950; Giddens 1991; Fukuyama 1995; Sztompka 1999, 2007; Hardin 2002; Uslaner 2002; Luhmann 2017). Nevertheless, in the categorical structures of philosophical reflection on cognition, knowledge, and communication, the category of trust did not appear at all. It was only due to the already mentioned conceptual shifts in confronting the philosophical problems experienced in the 20th century that questions about the role of trust in the knowledge-creating processes slowly emerged, and due to another path (the one that allowed for the discovery of the illocutionary force of the communication acts), also the possibility of questions about the place of trust in the structure of the communication relation (Wittgenstein 1969; Putnam 2000, 2001).

The analyses of the communication processes conducted in this respect naturally refer to all those interpersonal and social dimensions which, as a rule, are based on trust and which, as the research of psychologists and sociologists shows, absolutely require trust (Sztompka 2007). However, more and more consistently, these analyses reveal that it is the communicative situation that is the incubator of trust, similarly to the way it is in the case of mutualism and co-intentionality. Here, also, a kind of feedback takes place. Obligations, claims, and duties (the set of them—as accompanying knowledge—introduced into the performative layer of the communication act) only exist on the basis of trust in the ability and the possibility to relate to them and fulfill them. At the same time, the necessity to respect obligations (under the threat of a performative self-contradiction and thus losing the possibility of cooperation and falling out of discursive rationality) constantly strengthens the need for trust; strengthens trust itself; and, in some circumstances, builds it anew. These reciprocally complementary dependencies, which determine the dynamics of the communication relation, represent the inalienable coupling between communication cooperation and trust.

Nonetheless, this is coupling of a special nature. Its specificity results primarily from the fact that, as the transcendental-pragmatic analyses of the communication acts allow for concluding, at a deep level, that trust within the communication relation relates not so much to its participants as to the mechanisms that organize and consolidate this relation. This is, in a way, trust in the functioning of the communication relation itself, in the possibility of cooperation, and, above all, in the possibility of understanding (essential for it). This indubitably also includes trust in its participants, but it also has a specific character, because, to put it simply, it is trust that they will "fit into" the structure of this relation and all its requirements, that they will be well-functioning "links." It is precisely trust that makes it possible for the whole, that is, a given communicative situation, to function. The fact that collaborative understanding is even possible, it seems, is a rudimentary form of trust. Therefore, at this fundamental level, trust is an attitude in the communicative situation that not only determines participation in it but also aims unequivocally toward reaching understanding.

To some extent, this idea can be found in some research experiments focused on the reconstruction of human cognitive evolution, especially in ontogenetic order. Interesting inspirations in this respect are, for example, behind the construction of the "transactional self" proposed by Jerome Bruner (1986) or the "interpersonal self" distinguished by Ulric Neisser (1988) and his intuitions regarding the dimension that is determined as proto-communication. Nonetheless, they can also be found in the research and analyses of the mechanisms for respecting social norms and assuming status roles conducted by Tomasello (2009) or in extensive experiments tracking the manifestations of altruism and competition (for resources) among children and selected primates. These studies seem to confirm—however, always only marginally—that involvement in the communication relation and the cooperation undertaken within it are invariably determined by trust in the possibility of cooperative understanding. They seem to confirm, at least to some extent, the conviction that the primary matrix of trust understood as "a bet on uncertain future actions of other people" (Sztompka 2007, pp. 69–70) is trust in the functioning of the communication relation that is orientated toward understanding. Therefore, also at this level, trust can be understood as a kind of a bet, a bet on uncertain future circumstances—only that it is about uncertainty as to whether the communication relation will exist at all (it could be said: "it will sync" together with all its "links"), whether as such it can succeed.[8] This trust in the mechanisms of the functioning of communication cooperation just becomes a source and, in a way, a basis of trust in its participants.

At any level, however, trust remains an attitude that cannot be eliminated from the communicative context. Consequently, for each of these levels—exactly as for mutualism and co-intentionality—it is imperative to provide the conditions for its maintenance. Moreover, each of these requirements is a necessary pillar of discursive rationality.

## Notes

1 Some of them, including those resulting from the strict reflection procedure, are discussed in Chapter 6.
2 The anthropological perspective is a type of a research approach, according to which the actual (and real) subject of social sciences and humanities research are sets of activities and institutionalized human behavior, conceptualized as culturally shaped practices of the social community.
3 It is quite a surprise that the line of Kantian transcendental dialectics was most consistently developed by two apparently extremely different concepts, that is, the philosophy of Theodor W. Adorno and Ludwig Wittgenstein, neither of which places itself in the Kantian trend (it might be said: that's the charm of philosophical twists and turns!).
4 This distinction is discussed in Chapter 6.
5 The domain of Michael Tomasello's concepts and research (conducted for many years in cooperation with his teams) is exceptionally wide and covers issues within developmental psychology, linguistics, psychology of communication, primatology, evolutionary anthropology, comparative psychology, and philosophy—including mainly cognitive science.
6 The issue of normativity is further discussed in Chapters 8 and 9.
7 The distinction "proto-communication–communication" was discussed in Sierocka 2012.
8 By analogy with how (in Austin's nomenclature) an act of speech may or may not be successful.

# 6 Rigor of Discursive Rationality

Communication philosophy, due to the fact that it is set in the transcendental-pragmatic perspective and supported on pillars provided by non-philosophical theories and research related to communication cooperation, has theoretical tools of exceptional value. These are amazingly versatile tools. They can be used in a variety of different theoretical contexts and in connection with a variety of research perspectives. But, above all, their great value is that they can be applied to the majority of the most difficult traditional philosophical problems and the most recent ones. One such problem, which is firmly embedded in the history of philosophical and sociological thought, is that of rationality. In fact, this problem entails a whole, huge complex of issues, questions, and theoretical "dilemmas" that are in various ways related to human rationality.

Rationality is a subject matter we find in the oldest testimonies of philosophical reflection and invariably situated at its center, whatever different form it has taken. This is an absolutely key issue in handling the phenomena of megamedia aggression. Nonetheless, as is very common in philosophy, especially with regard to issues of the greatest importance, one of the particularly difficult tasks associated with it is specifying the supreme category itself, that is, clarifying what is hidden behind the question of rationality.

Indubitably, there is no place here for an even random presentation of these very complex disputes and resolutions as to what rationality is, or even how to understand the category itself. However, it should be pointed out that when philosophy inquires about rationality, it does not ask about **what we think** about the world, about ourselves, and about our actions and functioning in the world and among others. It does not ask about our comprehensive view of the world (even though rationality is manifested ultimately in these contents). However, in inquiring about rationality, philosophy raises questions about **how** and **in what way we think about it**;

how and according to what patterns we organize reality and our relations with it and our social behavior; according to what principles, in what way, and based on what we create the meaning; and how we assign goals. It asks what the evaluation mechanisms are, what the assessment matrices are and from where they come, and what methods we use to legitimize or justify certain social behaviors and actions. Therefore, the question about rationality is not so much about what we know as how and in what way we shape this knowledge or what intellectual ways we use to make the world understandable. It is not about how we act or how we behave but about how our knowledge justifies and legitimizes these behaviors and makes them understandable. Thus, in the most general terms (and, at the same time, with a large dose of disinvoltura), rationality is a coherent complex of intellectually "mastering" reality, determining our way of functioning in it.

The question about rationality, then, has extraordinary "specific gravity." And, in struggling with constructing the concepts of rationality, philosophy must primarily fulfill one basic condition: it must take a precisely defined theoretical position (being open to the hints of various external perspectives). However, this does not make this task for philosophy easier, as difficulties inevitably arise.

The more valuable turns out to be the perspective in which the concept of rationality is embedded in transcendental-pragmatic communication philosophy. The basic move that determined the rank of the concept of rationality developed by TP was the transformation of Kant's transcendentalism, which precisely specified theoretical position of TP. In fact, this transformation is a theoretical decision composed of four separate steps. The first is the indication taken from Kant's theory that the overriding philosophical problem is the question about the legitimation of knowledge and therefore not its authenticity, but its legitimacy (which is a shift that is extremely serious in consequences). The second step is to adopt Kant's opinion, according to which the guarantors of the legitimation of knowledge are transcendental, *a priori* knowledge-creating structures. According to this approach, the *a priori* conditions of the legitimacy of knowledge themselves pertain to its structure (and this approach, as we know, was a Kantian discovery, which he himself considered a breakthrough comparable to the Copernican revolution). In the third step, TP makes its own "revolutionary" discovery. It places the legitimation procedure in communicative *a priori*, which, certainly, has its justification in recognizing the communicative mediation of knowledge. Finally, there is the fourth step. The discovery by TP of the rank of communicative *a priori* entails a radical change in the legitimation procedure itself: here it takes the form of, as has already been said, the procedure described as "strict reflection." This procedure leads to the recognition that the *a priori,* transcendental, and therefore uncircumventable, framework of the knowledge-creating processes is determined by the formal structures of the communication acts (as essentially argumentative). The recognition of this dependence is a definite "novelty," not only in terms of Kant's philosophy but also in confrontation with the entire non-Kantian tradition.

This "novelty" could take place only because the legitimation procedure took into account, unprecedentedly, the dual, performative-propositional structure of linguistic acts (always communicative and always argumentative, which is demonstrated precisely by this procedure). Taking this duality into consideration made it possible to recognize that non-problematized knowledge accompanying the propositional layer, introduced into the performative layer, is knowledge relating to the conditions of the possibility of the argumentative consensus. And, in the strictly reflexive[1] legitimizing procedure, it was possible to demonstrate that any involvement in the communicative situation (relation, cooperation) was equivalent to accepting the validity of the argumentation rules, which set the framework for the possibility of any communication cooperation and, in fact, every single act of communication. This coupling of the reflexive and transcendental dimensions ultimately leads to the unquestionable deduction that the argumentative situation is uncircumventable (German: *unhintergehbar*)[2] and that the definitive conditions for the possibility of knowledge are determined by **presuppositions of argumentation**.

Demonstrating the impossibility of circumventing the argumentative situation is a **strictly reflexive** procedure, and therefore non-regressive, and, in this sense, absolutely definitive, because unlike all other schemes of definitive justification, it does not require acceptance of any external content. It comes down to recognizing that what is *implicit* in the act of argumentation is **always and forever** included.

This, in turn, to repeat, is conditioned by the duality of the structure of each linguistic act of communication. This duality means that the act is immanently present (in its performative layer) with obligations, claims, and presuppositions, which determine whether the act implemented by formulating the propositional content is successful or not and thus make it possible. Arguing, in the most fundamental sense, is invoking arguments in relation to those *implicitly* introduced obligations, claims, and duties. As such, argumentation pertains immanently to language, and in view of the linguistic constitution of knowledge, it shapes knowledge-creating tools. It is a constitutive moment of human *logos*.

This peculiar compulsion to argue, the inalienable involvement in argumentativeness, determines the specificity of our rationality. "Discursive argumentation" or discursiveness,[3] that is, argumentation directed at presuppositions immanently brought by the acts of communication, is the inalienable aspect of rationality. In procedural terms, discursiveness is indicated as a separate "level" of rationality (somewhat misleadingly referred to as discursive rationality; however, this is the definition that should remain). There are five such levels in TP: (1) mathematical and logical rationality, (2) technical and scientific rationality, (3) strategic rationality, (4) consensual and communicative rationality, and (5) discursive rationality (Apel 1986). However, the status of discursive rationality is definitely unique because, as it has already been suggested, the status of discursiveness is exceptional: it is not just one of many games that constitute our rationality but rather a transcendental game. Therefore, it is a game determining the *a priori* framework of rationality and its limits, and definitively determining the conditions of human rationality.

The conclusion here is unequivocal: discursiveness, as immanently inscribed in rationality, is essential for our communication practices. Every case of conflict or even ambiguities as to the validity of duties, obligations, and claims on which the construction of the ideal consensus is based, requires consideration of the argumentative discourse. And, at the same time, it is the idea of the unlimited consensus, as a synonym for the ideal communication community,[4] that requires maintaining communication cooperation within the limits of the argumentative discourse. Intellectual procedures cannot refer to any external, superior authority, as no such authority exists. They find no support anywhere outside. The argumentative discourse is the only tool that can, and should, be entrusted with the task of constructing, and, thus, legitimizing our rationality. Rationality absolutely requires discursiveness; in fact, it is essentially discursive.

Nonetheless, discursiveness is not simply "given" to our rationality. It would be more appropriate to say that it is **ASSIGNED** to us. Being, as TP calls it, a "transcendental function of reason" (Apel 1996, p. 30), it is realized only under conditions of real striving for the ideal consensus of the unlimited communication community. This is the essence of communication cooperation. Anticipating the unlimited definitive consensus (as the situation in which there is no longer a need to problematize claims, obligations, and duties), and the constant "confrontation" of the real communication community with the anticipated ideal form of it, are the indispensable requirements with which discursive rationality confronts us. Without meeting them, we ruin rationality. We ruin our social environment, that is, the real communication community, which is fundamentally dependent on the level of discursive rationality. The more numerous and frequent the situations that violate these requirements are, the weaker is the tissue of discursive argumentation, the more serious is the threat to rationality, and the more severe is the mutilation of the real communication community. Communicative aggression plays a specific role in these destructive processes.

Communicative aggression, in all its forms, destroys the cooperative link, which is the *sine qua non* condition for striving for the consensus. It undermines the *a priori* obligation to consensually agree on communication presuppositions as to their validity. It makes it impossible to stay within the framework set by argumentative discourse. All this strikes at the essence of discursive rationality as a transcendental game in which the communication community is involved. This is happening all the time on a smaller or larger scale. And it is always a disadvantage. It is always dangerous to the cohesiveness of our rationality. Especially the reality of the 20th century, characterized by Theodor Adorno and Max Horkheimer (1947)—unfortunately, extremely accurately—as a return of barbarism in the era of the "enlightened spirit," gave solid reasons for fearing the stability of our rationality. And, in terms of the problem of media aggression, this fear is all the more justified, as the sudden boom of mass media (in the first half of the 20th century) significantly contributed to destroying its stability. The rapid and unexpectedly effective totalizing of media systems (Siebert 1956) and the resulting powerful force of mass media played an extraordinary role in spreading 20th-century totalitarian regimes and in perpetuating the barbarism of our era. Nonetheless, today the situation is much more dangerous because the whole range of the previously existing means and practices of mass media (i.e., those which contributed to the 20th-century destruction of rationality) have been joined by completely new phenomena. These are phenomena of both a social and a psychological nature, and technological and ideological, all closely related to the reality of media. The whole configuration has contributed to a new reality, a megamedia reality, which, as we have seen, is hugely complicated, very expansive, highly influential, and highly unpredictable (mainly due to its extraordinary dynamics). Most importantly, this whole is the world in which communicative aggression has become an extremely serious threat to the rationality formed in a communicative way—and therefore a truly deadly threat to the communication community and to humanity itself.

What exactly makes the situation so particularly dangerous in terms of megamedia communication? What prompts such alarmist diagnoses in relation to the phenomena of megamedia aggression? And what justifies such radical postulates, such as those that are formulated here? Collecting the research findings so far, it can be said that megamedia aggression consists of a number of separate factors, each of which—albeit to a different degree and in a different way—participates in the process of destroying human rationality. Each makes its contribution to exacerbating this destruction.

Briefly recapitulating the previous findings, it should be said that, first of all, the alarmist tone of these diagnoses is justified, in the first place, by the fact that media aggression, in all its forms, prevents the obligation that is crucial for communication cooperation and annihilates the fundamental duty of striving for consensus. Thus, it destroys the idea of the unlimited communication community (as a synonym of the ideal consensus), which is superior to the argumentative discourse. And thus preventing the argumentative discourse, it destroys the conditions of the possibility of discursive rationality. The resulting threats to the communication community are of the highest importance, as they reach the very essence of its existence.

Second, the scale of threats to which discursive rationality is exposed from communicative aggression is influenced by basically all the characteristics of megamedia communication, including, to a very large extent, its total character (i.e., its presence in all spheres and dimensions of the contemporary world) and its global scope (i.e., the availability of communication events without time and space constraints). This means that aggression and its consequences also gain a total and global character, which, by all means, clearly translates into the level of its destructiveness.

Moreover, all the characteristics that comprise the new megamedia communication space also make it possible to provide within it full, unlimited communication, which could not take place in the reality of mass media. In the megamedia space, communication could emerge in the form it takes in situations not mediated by the media. It could be said: real communication. Surprisingly, this situation, although in many respects exceptionally beneficial and "promising," definitely increases our vulnerability to the destructive force of communicative aggression. As long as media messages allowed only a substitute for real communication relations, which was the situation in the era of analog mass media, the role of media in relation to aggression was essentially to propagate the attitudes, behaviors, and ideologies marked by it (which certainly significantly contributed to the hecatomb of the 20th-century totalitarian regimes). But when, in the reality of megamedia, these limitations were removed, when this reality made communication mediated by the media acquire all its constitutive characteristics such that it became real communication, the media space began to function as a specific arena in which, due to aggression, total and global in its scope, the fundamental structure of the communication relation began to undergo destruction and discursive rationality, the binder of the real communication community, together with it. Also, since almost all communication relations are gradually transferred to the megamedia sphere (or at least are mediated by it), the effect of this destruction is intensifying to an unprecedented degree.

Additionally, every form of media aggression strikes against the claims, obligations, and duties that are inherent in the communicative situation and condition it. Those which oblige to the reciprocal recognition of co-partnership, freedom of decision-making, efficiency in the assessment of argumentative strategy, independence in evaluation, or intellectual coherence are particularly severely affected. Undermining them always violates the dignity or freedom of the communication participants. At the same time, it makes it difficult or even impossible to establish a successful communication relation.

And, although these presuppositions are always counterfactual, and therefore they are not eligible here and now, the crux of the problem lies in the fact that aggression not only breaks and eliminates presuppositions but (which is crucial here), at the same time, prevents the fundamental duty that is the condition of their restitution: it prevents the obligation to the consensus. Thus, the chance to restore violated presuppositions is lost, and so is the chance to implement the "natural" course of the communication processes, which requires spreading them along the line "real–ideal communication community." Only in this mode can we manage to stay within rationality.

Furthermore, neither mutualism, nor co-intentionality, let alone trust, are immunized to the consequences of the destructive power of communicative aggression. And, at the same time, the scale of aggression in the megamedia space calls into question the possibility of meeting the rigors that result from them. Behind mutualism, co-intentionality, and trust, there are ideas that unambiguously oblige to these duties, norms, and values, which determine the content of validity claims to normative rightness.[5] It is equally clear that these ideas are undermined by the phenomena of megamedia aggression, which is a consequence of aggression breaking fundamental communication duties. Therefore, again, we are facing the situation in which aggression triggers a certain "spiral" process that is strongly detrimental to the processes of communication cooperation and, consequently, threatens the coherence and integrity of discursive rationality (and therefore the real communication community).

Finally, it is necessary to mention the issues that have not yet been addressed here, which are very extensive and important both due to the problem of aggression itself (not only in its communicative manifestations) and to questions about the condition of our rationality (not only with regard to the threat of aggression). We are talking here about the phenomena of exclusion, stigmatization, and discrimination as well as their peculiar "reverse," which is the "compulsion of identity."[6] In terms of these phenomena, the complex of issues raised by researchers of various scientific disciplines gives a fairly clear (and, in fact, highly alarmist) picture of the multiple interrelations between what can be described precisely as the "compulsion of identity," and acts of exclusion, stigmatization and discrimination, and the phenomena of aggression. Aggression observed in the megamedia space sharpens this image, but due to it, it sends even clearer warning signals and allows for a better understanding of its role in devastating our rationality.

However, strictly speaking, this is exactly the purpose of the identification of all the circumstances listed here. They all caution about the seriousness of the situation we are facing as the communication community "thrown" into the new, megamedia space. All of them testify that the specific shape of the megamedia world, with its innovative, mostly very valuable characteristics, make aggression—invariably accompanying communicative situations—the main factor not only destroying the stability of the communication relations but also (and, in fact, primarily) destroying the stability of the foundations of rationality, which is essentially discursive. Consequently, megamedia aggression becomes a factor that makes it impossible to maintain the stability of the communication community. There are definitely, as has been discussed more broadly, many other negative phenomena that have emerged with the new media space or have taken on a new, hardly acceptable shape with it. Nevertheless, it is aggression that plays the inglorious role of this force, which, under the conditions of megamediality, is able to interfere with the formal structures that condition communication cooperation and is capable of destroying them. Unsettling the foundations of rationality, destroying stability, or even threatening the existence of the communication community are "just" consequences of this destructive interference.

## Notes

1 The reflexive procedure is understood here (in line with the etymology of the term) as a self-referential procedure, a self-directed behavior. It is therefore reflection that makes use of what it is itself. The reflexive legitimation procedure is a procedure that in no step goes beyond the structure itself. In particular, it does not confront the objective sphere. As a clearly distinguished argumentative strategy, reflection appears for the first time in works of Descartes. The second significant project based on it is Kantianism. And finally, it appears in TP in the form of strict reflection—"strict," that is, free from the inconsistencies that occurred in the works of both Descartes and Kant.
2 In transcendental pragmatics, this key thesis translates into three statements, or more precisely, it is said to be a conjunction of the following three statements:

> (1) We cannot meaningfully, that is, without contradicting, question the rules and presuppositions of meaningful argumentation; (2) We cannot rationally, that is, without falling into *petitio principii*, justify these rules and presuppositions; (3) We cannot rationally, that is, by not recognizing them at least *implicitly,* decide against their justification.
> 
> (Kuhlmann 1981, p. 15)

3 See Chapter 4.
4 To realize the importance of the postulate of the definitive consensus of the unlimited communication community, it is worth noting that in the construction of TP, it replaces the Kantian transcendental unity of apperception, which is the "peak" of the transcendental deduction of principles.
5 See Chapter 8.
6 A brief discussion on these issues is included in Chapter 9.

# Part III
# Ethics of Media Communication

# 7 Public Responsibility of the Media

Already at the stage of early research on mass communication (in the 1940s), questions were raised about the mechanisms hidden in the media space that destroy the stability of our rationality. These were also questions about the factors that would allow for restoring its integrity and regaining trust in it. Although these questions were rarely asked directly, there was clearly a growing awareness that rationality, as a complex of intellectual tools and structures that conditions; organizes; and adds meaning, goals, and values to our functioning in reality (in its biological, social, institutional, and cultural dimensions), absolutely must be protected against the danger it is exposed to in the media space. No matter how deep the destruction of rationality may be, the most serious threats are invariably associated with—the history of the 20th century left no doubts about it.

For various reasons (often determined by even contradictory interests of a social or political nature), it turned out that it was necessary to undertake research on media systems, which ultimately gave insights regarding the threats and the possible protection of rationality. Gradually, a model of public responsibility of the media emerged from this and slowly began to focus on the entire set of duties that the media would take over to try to ensure such protection. Thus, the question about responsibility eventually became the most serious and important issue in media practice and media theory.

The definitions of the term "responsibility" reveal two main meanings. First, to be responsible for something is to take the blame for deeds, actions, reprehensible conditions, and situations that bring harm and, consequently, to be punished for that (to bear the consequences of (not) taking these actions, or even just the occurrence of certain situations). Responsibility understood in this way is a "moral or legal obligation."

In the second sense, to be responsible for someone or something is to accept the obligation to take care of that someone or something, or to provide conditions for the implementation of something.

In fact, these two definitions compose a third meaning, which seems the most appropriate in relation to the model of public responsibility of the media. In this third sense, responsibility is to care for something, while at the same time accepting (voluntarily or not) the consequences, both favorable and unfavorable, that result from the success or failure of this care. Responsibility realized in this way builds, within the conscious communication community, the conditions for the transformation into co-responsibility (as revealed by communication philosophy, and outlined below).

With regard to the media, the first meaning of "responsibility" is related to the fact that, due to the type of activity the media engage in, they are burdened with codified legal liability, both criminal and civil, as well as with professional liability. However, certainly, apart from the legal obligation to "be responsible for one's own or someone else's actions," there is also a moral obligation. In this regard, not all aspects of media responsibility are regulated by law, and not all are even covered by the provisions of professional codes. These codes, if assessed from the perspective of philosophical demands, suffer from a fundamental deficiency. For the most part, they lack a solid foundation in a coherent, universal ethical system, although such systems are available.

In the second sense, responsibility—although constantly taking different shades—is always somehow related to the attitude that requires serious and careful concentration on a matter, object, or person, with a commitment to achieve the desired (and anticipated) result. It is also characteristic that we assign responsibility understood in this way to subjects that we simultaneously perceive as reliable and trustworthy. The subjects to whom such responsibility can be attributed include the media. And although the theoreticians and researchers of the media have not always paid strict attention to the category of responsibility, most research and resolutions have oscillated around this idea of its meaning.

This perception of responsibility was introduced into media research by the famous so-called "Hutchins Report," *A Free and Responsible Press* (published over 70 years ago). Contrary to its title, this report does not only concern the press. As Robert Hutchins declared in his introduction, the content of the report covers the entire spectrum of the media, among which the author mentioned "radio, newspapers, film, magazines, and books" (Commission on

Freedom of the Press 1947). It seems that this document is already very historical and therefore not very relevant. This is partly how it can be assessed because there are undoubtedly many aspects that are out-of-date. Nevertheless, both entirely and in detail, the report demonstrates in an interesting way how many problem layers constitute the responsibility that should be assigned to the media. It also unequivocally reveals that the aforementioned general perception of the category of "responsibility" ultimately says little about how to understand, implement, and evaluate it in the mediasphere. In short, it highlights the powerful problems (of both a practical and theoretical nature) that are associated with the implementation of the model of public responsibility of the media.

The declared intention of the report, and the research that preceded it, was to reflect on the condition of media freedom of that time and the prospects of freedom for the future. The category of freedom is placed here—partly in line with the long philosophical tradition—in three distinct semantic contexts: freedom from, freedom for, and media-specific freedom to. The analyses concerning it focus on two sets of issues: first, on identifying the groups of factors that limit or might potentially limit the freedom and independence of the media, and, second, on identifying those activities that are meant to prevent the misuse of the acquired freedom by the media (it can be said: the effects that result from its irresponsible use, from its dangerous overuse). With regard to both of these sets, the report seems to clearly show that the main line on which most of the problems are located here is the "freedom–responsibility" tension. The effort to capture the most important determinants that allow for maintaining the relative balance between freedom and responsibility is, it seems, the most important and most valuable feature of this document. Ultimately, this translates into suggestions regarding the mechanisms of media self-regulation, as well as the recognition of the duties and demands that a free society requires from the media, which is written in the report in the famous five ideal demands that define the foundations of the emerging doctrine of public responsibility of the media.[1]

As Hutchins himself judged, the postulates formulated by the report are neither particularly new nor surprising. There is also nothing extraordinary about them. The demands and duties that are advocated to the media here are simply obvious and indisputable. Despite their obviousness, however, they are still very current postulates that require implementation. Thus, in an unanticipated way, they still remain in the declarative sphere. Another less-than-pleasant surprise is the fact that the report did not actually attract the attention of media practitioners. For many years, in fact, only a few theorists referred to its content, because only a few attempted to deal with the problem of media responsibility (e.g., Gerald 1963, in Bertrand 1997).

However, irrespective of these circumstances, the report permanently highlights responsibility as a fundamental duty of the media and a basic "weapon" that can strengthen our rationality in the media space and protect against its destruction. And, although it took a long time to comprehensively assume this approach, never again, neither in media practice nor in media theory, could the rank of responsibility be questioned, much less challenged. This happened despite the questions, to this day, about what it really is, what it should be, where the sanctions legitimizing it come from, how to enforce it, and how to "fight for it." The times in which the report was produced quite obviously confronted the problem of responsibility along with the issue of freedom, exposing the self-regulation of the media and their self-discipline in using the freedoms acquired as the proper expression of "new public responsibility." However, socio-political and media constellations that changed over time gradually revealed that, first of all, the problem of responsibility has to be associated with a much broader and richer complex of commitments and duties (which was best implemented by the project of Claude-Jean Bertrand), and, second, that this problem is essentially closely correlated to the foundations of the ethical doctrine (which clearly shows the transcendental-pragmatic project of communication philosophy). Naturally, this does not mean losing sight of the need to "monitor freedom and independence of the media." Nonetheless, the severity of the problem is visibly shifting.

In the project of Claude-Jean Bertrand—proposed almost 50 years after the Hutchins Report and clearly marking another important stage in media research on responsibility—the line of tensions no longer runs between responsibility and freedom (Bertrand 1997). It is replaced, in fact, by the "responsibility–trust" relation. In the tension between them, a fundamental game is taking place, a game in which the media take part on the one hand, and legal regulations and market rules are closely involved on the other hand, while everything takes place in front of and for an audience, which are the media users. It is appropriate to ask each of these participants about their perception of trust in the media, as each is exposed to the effects of excessive trust and has to work out the methods for gaining and maintaining social trust. What occupied Bertrand most is the question about how the media can secure necessary public trust. The answer is simply that trustworthy media are reliable media; it is in their efforts toward and care of reliability that their responsibility is expressed. The implementation of responsibility is to be ensured, on the one hand, by a deontology project and, on the other hand, by a multi-point system of media responsibility, that is, the famous system of media accountability (M*A*S). The deontology project is, according to Bertrand, a complex of principles and rules developed in the media environment, focused on the social functioning of the media and aimed at improving the quality of media services. On the other hand, M*A*S is a set of activities, procedures, and projects, as well as institutions, ideas, and strategies which, while safeguarding the integrity of the media, enable the fulfillment of the duties included in the deontology project.

Such a comprehensive approach, as contained in Bertrand's concept, shows the complicated nature of the "machine" in which the mechanisms of public responsibility are involved. This concept also indicates that the enormous amount of work from the media is required to construct both the deontological project and the system of factors enabling its implementation, and thus to fulfill the most important duty, which is maintaining social trust. Despite the advantages of Bertrand's project—not to be overestimated and indeed widely appreciated both in the media environment and among media researchers—Bertrand's concept forces further theoretical steps. These steps are important because of both the necessity of a solid and unquestionable strengthening of the deontological content and the urgent need for the fullest possible involvement of the media in activities aimed not only at promoting stable rationality but also at creating and securing discursiveness, which is a necessary condition for this stability.

Bertrand was aware of the extraordinary rank of the media. He wrote directly that "the fate of all mankind" depends on improvement of the media and argued that "only democracy can (...) ensure the survival of civilization, and without well-informed citizens there is no democracy; there are no enlightened citizens without high-quality media" (Bertrand 1997, p. 7). This theorist clearly formulated the opinion that the duties of the media "come from the right of every human being to accurate, comprehensive, understandable and useful information." Moreover, pointing to the tools and methods that, as part of self-regulation, the responsible media should use to improve themselves and thus ensure social trust, he ascribes to the media a very wide range of commitments, both in terms of prevention and enforcement mechanisms, and, finally, effective sanctions. All of this testifies to the serious and extraordinary role assigned to the media by Bertrand's project, but in no way does it exclude the necessity to take the next theoretical steps suggested above. These steps have to provide definitive answers to questions about fundamental deontological sanctions and arguments that defend rationality, in order to guarantee both the tools and premises necessary to defend rationality against the media aggression that is today so "deadly" for it.

In the quarter of a century since Bertrand's project, little has changed in the general theoretical approach to media responsibility and responsibility required from the media (McQuail 2003; Plaisance 2000). Also, within the scope of the practical activities carried out in the media environment—largely following the indications mentioned in M*A*S—public responsibility of the media is perceived as identical to the self-regulatory procedures intended to increase the quality of media services and strengthen social trust in the media, which consequently help in meeting important social needs. All this is achieved by intentionally established institutions, developed documents, constructed tools, and implemented methods. The most popular among them (found almost universally, although undoubtedly not in countries enslaved by regimes) are program councils, press councils, councils on ethics, news/media housing, codes of professional conduct, arbitration by fellow workers, developed ways of contacting receivers, public debates on media activity, and critical analyses of their activities.[2] The digitization and networking of media communication transferred some of these activities to the cyberspace, which greatly intensified some of them[3] but did not fundamentally change their nature (Urbaniak 2011). All these solutions can be very effective at improving the work of the media; they contribute to their reliability and undoubtedly create numerous opportunities to design effective forms of resistance in counteracting aggression. Nonetheless, these solutions also suffer from very serious limitations. These limitations can be seen as "inherited" from the concept of public responsibility of the media, which, while determining the most mature model of mass media functioning (and, at the same time, the most complicated model), still requires very important complements and some important corrections. These complements are also absolutely necessary because it is the model of public responsibility of the media that is the only appropriate starting point in order to, by protecting the media, protect communication from the danger of destruction due to megamedia aggression, in which rationality is threatened to the greatest extent.

What makes it impossible (however, responsible) to undertake this type of "mission" and its fairly complete implementation is the lack of four fundamental elements in this model, or even the main pillars of this type of construction: namely, (1) the lack of embedding and strengthening responsibility in ethics; (2) the lack of arguments justifying ethical constructions; (3) the lack of justification of normativity itself (in relation to the developed model); and, in terms of all this, (4) the lack of coherent and legitimized critical tools. Apart from these four circumstances—at first glance purely theoretical but in fact strictly determining current media practices—one more important limitation remains: this model refers only to the reality of mass media communication. On the other hand, all these phenomena, which no longer fit into the media space and whose specific features constitute the characteristics of megamediality, are only marginally subject to the tools and methods developed and recommended within the traditional model of public responsibility. Nonetheless, it is not about the complete rejection or depreciation of these traditional tools and methods. Since the mass media space has been absorbed (and also modified to some extent) by the reality of megamedia, it is necessary for this new reality to partially adapt the traditional tools that have been constructed and employed to solve the problems constantly arising between responsibility and trust. These tensions do not disappear in the megamedia space but rather seem to be gaining in strength. However, it is very important that they are revealed here as tensions immanently resulting from the structure of the communication relation. Due to this, it is possible to finally see that responsibility actually has the status of the ethical principle, which is the fundamental principle.

The "litmus test" that undisputedly confirmed the timeliness of the tensions on the line "freedom–responsibility–trust," as well as revealed other powerful dilemmas of today's media reality, turned out to be—which is already firmly rooted in the new megamedia reality—the WikiLeaks case. Already with the first views of this site,[4] we dealt with phenomena that do not fit into the space defined by mass media practices, existing in the organizational; financial; political; psychological; and, above all, ethical dimensions. Posting on this portal, as it was announced by WikiLeaks, "original source materials," which documented very serious, complicated, and painful events (and therefore concealed or at least misrepresented to the public), assigned a completely new role to the receivers of the media message. The effort (but also the privilege) of selecting, interpreting, and evaluating the published content from materials from all corners of the globe relating to very diverse problems of the modern world fell to the receivers. They were also given the decisions as to the possible ways of using the acquired knowledge in practice. In this scenario, there was also the natural hope that by gaining this knowledge, the media receivers would gradually gain power and that the well-established but also clearly identified and ruthlessly exposed relations of knowledge and power (Foucault 1966, 1975b) would begin to undergo significant transformations. The fact that the materials published on WikiLeaks were obtained and compiled by volunteers not professionally related to journalism and the official media became a special advantage of these publications and began to function as a guarantor of their credibility. The WikiLeaks phenomenon significantly strengthened the belief that the media could be disentangled from its dependence on business and politics, and it also increased hope that real interference in the rigid structures of power was possible through public knowledge.

On the other hand, negotiations with powerful titles in the world press initiated by Julian Assange at some stage of his activity[5] and certain, though only partial, success of this cooperation revealed a kind of powerlessness and helplessness of media activity separated from the institutions and mechanisms of mass communication. They also revealed a bulk of dilemmas, of smaller or larger importance, that were almost impossible to resolve without prior fundamental (which does not mean dogmatic) resolutions.[6] The independence of the media message from involvement in the network of political interests turned out to be equally problematic. Above all was the issue of responsibility for the consequences of these involvements, as well as the issue of responsibility for numerous other aspects of media activity embodied by WikiLeaks, which is also related to citizen journalism, the blogosphere, and the social media. All these forms of media involvement in some way reopen the issue of responsibility. In fact, it is only they, as the most important centers of megamedia activity, that open up the chance to take real responsibility for the implementation of communication in the media space and thus for shaping communicative rationality. The megamedia space, generating a bulk of new problems, questions, and dilemmas, and, at the same time, dangerously increasing the threats of media aggression, simultaneously creates an unprecedented opportunity to shape a model (and with it also attitudes) of responsibility, which—falling within the scope of the third perception of the term "responsibility" mentioned here—can be a real guarantor of discursive rationality. And it will be thorough co-responsibility.

There is unconditionally a very serious opportunity for all of this, but it remains only an "opportunity" until we recognize it as a TASK, exactly as it relates to discursiveness itself. The implementation of this task, divided into countless individual projects, requires significant theoretical solutions at the initial stage, primarily in response to the shortcomings of the traditional model of media responsibility listed here. Consequently, the most important elements in this respect are (1) embedding and consolidating responsibility in the sphere of ethics, (2) definitively justifying ethical norms, (3) legitimizing normativity itself (demonstrating its possibility and necessity), and (4) developing coherent and justified critical tools. Outlining these steps (even as concise and brief as the one presented in the next chapter) complements the list of resolutions that define the basic framework of the design of communication philosophy and provide us with the theoretical tools without which we lose our chances in the clash with megamedia aggression.

## Notes

1 These recommendations state that in order for the media to respond to social needs and serve (as defined in the report) free society—while exercising freedom in a responsible manner—they have to (1) provide true, comprehensive, and intelligent coverage on the events of the day in a meaningful context, (2) constitute a forum for the exchange of comments, (3) provide a representative picture of all social groups, (4) have appropriate methods of presenting and explaining goals and values, and (5) guarantee full access to current information.
2 These practical activities are strongly supported by research projects (including international projects, such as *Media Accountability and Transparency in Europe* (*MediaAcT*) and *European Journalism Observatory*), which, among other values, have great potential to support self-regulatory media undertakings, both those carried out within a single country and those of a global nature.
3 Blogs (mainly those dedicated exclusively to media issues) as well as internet forums focused around specialized websites have the greatest share in the intensification of these activities (Urbaniak 2011).
4 WikiLeaks, launched by Julian Assange in 2006, put a million documents online in less than a year.
5 The negotiations concerned publishing materials at the disposal of Assange, among others, in *Der Spiegel*, *El Pais*, *Le Monde*, *New York Times*, *The Guardian*, and *The Times*.
6 The most difficult dilemmas arose, among others, when faced with questions about on what to base trust in knowledge obtained from outside traditional media sources, what expectations should be

formulated, how to enforce these expectations, what are the limits of freedom in disclosing potentially dangerous content, what are the chances of spontaneous, unregulated access to the sensitive content, how to bridge the gap between copyright and human rights, what threats and benefits are associated with the practices of "distribution" of knowledge (e.g., through gatekeeping or agenda setting), and what are possibilities of neutralizing these practices. These dilemmas—revealed in specific constellations due to WikiLeaks—signal problems of a very wide and general scope, problems directly related to the stability of communicative rationality (which is, as we remember, essentially discursive).

# 8 Co-responsibility

Due to the problem of aggression in the media space, the efforts of communication philosophy studies must culminate in findings that will allow for the constructed model of responsibility—which does not refer only to the mediasphere—to become a real guarantor of discursive rationality. And responsibility will entirely be co-responsibility.

For transcendental-pragmatic (TP) project, the starting point for the construction of such a model, as mentioned previously, is the recognition that the conditions for the constitution of rationality are determined by the fundamental structure of the communication relation, the specificity of which, in turn, results from the performative-propositional unity of the communication acts. For questions about responsibility, the most important consequence of this is that the content of claims and obligations (immanent in the performative layer of these acts) determines the conditions for the possibility of realizing the state of ideal agreement anticipated in them. It is a state in which there is a consensual agreement of claims and resulting norms, due to which they are no longer subject to further problematization. This state is defined, as we remember, as the ideal (or unlimited) communication community.

The ideal communication community—precisely as a regulative idea of human communication—is anticipated in every act of communication. This means that its anticipation is brought about by the real acts and, therefore, it takes place within the real communication community. It is also here, in the real community, that is, in the conditions for the indispensable, counterfactual anticipation of the ideal community, that our efforts to obtain consensual agreements as to the validity of claims and obligations are embedded and, thus, our efforts to realize the ideal communication community.

Thus, the ideal and the real community are engaged in a constant, specific game, especially because the former (the ideal community) is a transcendental condition for the possibility of the latter, and, at the same time, the former cannot be realized in the latter. We are invariably destined to be involved in this dialectical game. Moreover, in such a game, the human being is constituted as *homo communicativus*. Our communicative rationality and our efforts to maintain its discursiveness are shaped in this game.

It is this immanent tension between the real and the ideal community that **generates the ethical duty of responsible cooperation to maintain the conditions for the realization of the ideal communication community**. This duty is contained in the structural conditions of possible communication. Their detailed analysis—carried out by applying the method of "strict reflection"—ultimately allows for the formulation of basic ethical norms and imperatives, directly resulting from the specificity of communication cooperation, and obliging the communication participants to responsible participation in shaping the conditions that bring about the realization of the ideal community. These norms, although they seem to sound quite succinctly, with imperative power, oblige us to accept co-responsibility for eliminating the difference between the ideal and the real world (both in its micro and macro dimensions). What is even more important is that these norms also clearly indicate that the responsibility for overcoming the distance between the ideal and the real community is shared by all participants of the actually implemented communication process. Everyone takes co-responsibility!

The norms which "guard" our co-responsibility in the effort to overcome this distance, and which are its foundation, result from the argumentative situation itself, which is problematizing claims and obligations (and toward which we ask questions about what is right and what, as a consequence, we should do). As part of this argumentation (as the proper discourse), the will to find a proper resolution to a given problem is assumed and recognized as uncircumventable, which, for the time being, means the will toward rational argumentation. This clearly shows the content of the first norm discovered by TP, which takes the following form:

> "If we really seriously want to know something, if we are seriously interested in solving a given problem, then we are required (*ist geboten*) to strive by means of rational argumentation for the correct resolution" (Kuhlmann 1985b, p. 185). Dispensing with the conditional form of this norm, TP formulates it as a categorical imperative: "**Argue rationally!**

Both the content of the revealed norm and the wording of the imperative are potentially in the very essence of the argumentation procedure. They are a kind of normative explication of the fact that the argumentative situation remains—under the threat of performative self-contradiction—an uncircumventable situation; hence, their imperative and not merely hypothetical nature. Their absolutely binding force, the fact that they cannot be disregarded, allows their content to be qualified as normative. However, this content, due to its general nature, has to be completed. Its necessary detailing takes the form of successive norms for which the former, as the superior and most important one, invariably constitutes the essential reference.

This means, first of all, that this specific "categorical imperative" is an authoritative indication that argumentation can only take place within the communication community, that is, in the conditions of the indispensable, counterfactual anticipation of the unlimited (ideal) argumentative community. This leads to the conclusion that the content of the imperative generates the absolute validity of the norm with the following wording: "If we are seriously interested in solving a problem, we have to strive for such a resolution which anyone could accept, therefore we have to strive for the rational consensus" (Kuhlmann 1985b, p. 185).

This norm is connected with specific validity claims to assurance and absoluteness, truth, protection from doubt, allegations, and contradictions (Kuhlmann 1985a). This is simply due to the fact that rational consensus is conceptualized by TP as the fulfillment of these claims under the conditions of the unlimited argumentative community. According to the above norm, which can be expressed as another categorically formulated imperative—"**Strive for the rational consensus!**"—(Kuhlamnn 1985b, p. 189), the participants of argumentation are obliged to acknowledge all arguments supporting or undermining the certainty of the problematized content (and we know that we operate invariably at the level of argumentation *par excellence*, that is, relating to the issue the of standing of validity claims).

The imperative claim to the consensus implies that, as seriously arguing persons, we are obliged to serious cooperation with other participants in the argumentation process. By performing the act of communication, which is always arguing, the receiver is invariably made a cooperation proposal, which this receiver can take in various ways: accept, question, demand an argument, and so on. In any case, communication and argumentation take place only when the partner cooperatively responds to this offer in some way

(Kuhlamnn 1985b). Thus, serious participation in cooperation requires the partner of argumentation to be regarded as a subject capable of argumentative cooperation, which, in particular, means that this subject should be considered capable of truth and rational argument and, likewise, requires such recognition on the part of the partner. In the full sense, this is about recognizing the partner as equal in argumentation. It also means that the partner is considered capable of free argumentative choices, and that "limitless recognition of the freedom of the other" is assumed, which is also associated with a simultaneous claim to reciprocity. This situation of absolute reciprocal recognition (the recognition of reciprocal claims and the recognition of each other as persons) is an implied situation, or more precisely, contained in the imperative postulated in the second norm: "Strive for the rational consensus!"

The wording, which is undoubtedly pompous, can comprise the content stated by both these norms in such a way that being in the argumentative situation (invariably uncircumventable) is the requirement of the acceptance of argumentative laws and the recognition of the equality of the members of the argumentative community before these laws. And, since argumentation has—like every act of communication—the status of activity, this acceptance refers to practically relevant laws. Thus, the coherent complement of the second norm—as, in fact, the obligation to strive for the theoretical consensus—is the third norm, which is stated as: "Whenever your interests could collide with the interests of others, **strive for the rational, practical consensus** with them!" (Kuhlmann 1985b, p. 208).

This norm, much more complicated in its consequences and in its scope, and already encompassing the sphere of moral decisions and choices, results absolutely from the very (performative-propositional) structure of the linguistic acts and also (though in a different sense) absolutely refers to the reality of the real communication community. They are the actual starting point for it. Ultimately, these are the actions to which, through the imperative to unconditionally build the practical consensus, the content of this norm obliges. This is reflected in the last of four norms revealed in the transcendental-pragmatic analyses of the argumentative act, which reads: "**Always strive to contribute to the (long-term) realization of such relations that bring closer the achievement of the ideal communication community** and constantly ensure that the existing conditions for a possible realization of the ideal communication community are preserved!" (Kuhlmann 1985b, p. 214).

All these norms of rational argumentation and their associated imperative orders, which are constituted invariably from the perspective of the idea of the unlimited communication community, define the horizon of ethical duties. Their validity is guaranteed by the principle of performative non-self-contradiction, and this validity is based on a specific presupposition of the argumentative act, the unity of the form and the content. Nonetheless, as normative rules of argumentation, these norms maintain the character of formal rules. What makes them ethically relevant is, on the one hand, their unquestionable binding force (that cannot be denied under the threat of performative self-contradiction) and, on the other hand, their content reference to the sphere of interpersonal interactions and the real relations that determine them. As such, they are the foundation of ethics (initially defined in terms of TP as communication ethics, and gradually developed, by Apel and Habermas, as discourse ethics), constituting the only guarantor of "the survival of the human species as the real communication community" (Apel 1973, p. 431). The responsibility for assigning this rank cannot be transferred to any external authority because it is a consequence of our co-participation in the communication community and, as such, is our co-responsibility. It is co-responsibility resulting directly from the discursive nature of communicative rationality and, to put it metaphorically, from the structure of human conversation. Maintaining this "conversation" and ensuring the reality enabling it is a condition for maintaining the stability of our rationality. Therefore, it is also a condition for the possibility of maintaining the communication community, in which all its participants are co-responsible, and which is possible only when, through participation in rational argumentation, in consensual arrangements as to the validity of claims and obligations, and, above all, in striving for the rational consensus, the ethical norms imposed by the immanent structure of this "conversation" are respected. Co-responsibility—as a principle that imposes a commitment on us to cooperate in the construction of real relations, which would gradually eliminate the difference between the real and ideal state of the communication community—is therefore the highest duty to which we are obligated. It sets unambiguously the ethical foundation of specific human activities and thus determines the possible scope of the project of the ethics of co-responsibility.[1]

The fact that we are absolutely obligated to co-responsibility and, to put it somewhat metaphorically, destined to it as a fundamental ethical principle is determined not only by the specific, discursive structure of the acts of communication. Its indispensability results equally from numerous other circumstances, both those directly related to the remaining essential features of communication and those resulting from the real (historical and current) formations of our world, including its megamediality.

The duty of co-responsibility is already revealed at the level of mutualistic ties that bind the participants in the simplest act of communication cooperation. It is to a no lesser extent and no less strongly related to the phenomenon of co-intentionality. Both of these dimensions, which determine the unique nature of our communication competence, inevitably place our activities in a kind of common space determined by our shared activities, goals, and intentions and, consequently, by the values, norms, and principles they imply. All these aspects, this entire specific space—precisely because of the mutualistic ties and co-intentions—is a joint achievement, which naturally entails co-responsibility toward it. Thus, avoiding this co-responsibility, either consciously or involuntarily rejecting it (also as co-responsibility for ensuring the real conditions enabling the striving for the perfect consensus), is tantamount to breaking these mutualistic ties, to breaking the community of intentions. Ultimately, it simply means breaking the cooperation.

Co-responsibility for the success of communication (though not often realized by subjects of communication) also applies to its other dimensions. Its success or failure is not exhausted by the shortcomings that John Austin pointed out in such a revealing way. A successful communicative situation is not simply the sum of the individual successful speech acts. Counterfactual anticipation of the unlimited consensus (as the ideal communication community), maintaining the communication relation within the limits set by its *a priori* structure, maintaining the rigor of argumentative discourse, obeying the principle of performative non-self-contradiction, and, accordingly, operating and fulfilling obligations, claims, and duties are the restrictions that determine the success of communication cooperation. They are (and have to be!) the subject of co-responsibility of its participants. None of them separately have the responsibility for fulfilling (or striving to meet) these restrictions, and none of the participants in communication cooperation (unless it is deformed or faked cooperation) is the sole administrator of this responsibility. And yet, to refer once again to the quoted sentence of Hans-Georg Gadamer, it belongs to all of them and is borne jointly by everyone!

Many concepts, not only philosophical and not only ethical, have the principle of responsibility as the supreme ethical norm, as well as the idea of the ethics of responsibility supported by it. In fact, in each of them, the motive, and sometimes simply the impulse to expose responsibility (co-responsibility) or even ennoble it to the rank of the highest ethical principle, is the fear for the condition of our world, the fear of the processes of which we are the authors and in which we remain helpless, like a sorcerer's apprentice, knowing no magic spell to reverse their dangerous consequences. According to these concepts, the principle of responsibility seems to have power, however, probably not magical. And even more serious hopes should be associated here with the idea of co-responsibility.

In the opinions of the authors of philosophical concepts, which assigned a particularly wide scope to the ethical principle of responsibility or co-responsibility, the most troublesome sources of civilization anxiety include the uncontrolled technological progress, the multidimensional processes of globalization and their consequences, the threat of armed nuclear conflict, and the vision of a total ecological disaster (Apel 1973; Jonas 1979; Habermas 1981; Kuhlmann 1987; Böhler 1994). Non-philosophical theories, such as the quoted concept of public responsibility of the media or the deontology project associated with M*A*S, were, in turn, motivated in their search primarily by the fear of a total loss of trust in the media, or an even more serious danger of enslaving media by, for example, a dominant political power (ideological, religious), or by free market mechanisms. All these dangers, against which the doctrine of responsibility was engaged, were joined by the threat of very serious destruction of the stability of the entire space of communication, adapted by megamedia and therefore exposed to unprecedented dangers from media aggression. The diagnosed and anticipated consequences of these threats, that is, the destruction of the fundamental conditions for the existence of the real communication community and the destruction of stability of our rationality, seem to obligate us to assume universal co-responsibility for the phenomena observed in this new (or at least radically changed) media space. And, above all, they obligate us to assume co-responsibility toward the aggression observed in this space, because it is aggression, as has been shown, that constitutes a fundamental threat here. Moreover, and importantly, taking over co-responsibility for protecting (or even defending) rationality is not a question of political choice, ideological declarations, or religious views (although they are also decisive here). It is simply a matter of submitting to the rigors of discursive rationality within which and due to which our functioning is possible that the existence of the real communication community is possible. Only as much, and yet so much!

The requirement to submit to the rigors of discursive rationality, resulting from concern for the state of the modern world, and, most importantly, well-established by deriving the principle of co-responsibility from the ethics project, gains another theoretical reinforcement due to the already announced possibility of subjecting this project to the procedure of definitive justification. This procedure was constructed by TP on the basis of specific transcendental argumentation, presented in the most mature form by Immanuel Kant. However, due to its regressive nature, and the fact that Kant based this procedure on the unreliable interference of the conditional period and on assumptions whose content maintains at most a hypothetical value, the formula of this argumentation had to be transformed. Due to the procedure, which is referred to in TP as "strict reflection,"[2] it was transformed into an unconditional and imperative argument, invariably applied to the Kantian "What can I know?" question. The difference, however, is that the procedure constructed by TP, apart from the rigor of strict reflection, also differs from the Kantian proposal in the sense that it is directed not at the problem of possible experience but at the question of argumentation. Thus, the proper subject of this procedure becomes the possibility of the validity of the rules of sensible argumentation, which, after reformulation, comes down to the problem of the possibility of the validity of presuppositions inherent in the argumentative act.

Ultimately, it is the procedure that reveals the definitive impossibility of circumventing the argumentative situation. The situation of a reasonably arguing person is uncircumventable, as it is impossible to question any of the three parts of the conjunction into which the argument is translated. We are talking here, to recall, about the conjunction of the following tasks:

> (1) We cannot meaningfully, that is, without contradicting, question the rules and presuppositions of meaningful argumentation; (2) We cannot rationally, that is, without falling into *petitio principii,* justify these rules and presuppositions; and (3) We cannot rationally, that is, by not recognizing them at least *implicitly,* decide against their justification.[3]
> (Kuhlmann 1981, p. 15)

Thus, the definitive justification procedure reveals that the validity of ethical norms (and the imperatives that conclude them) is confined within the framework of argumentation, and what determines the definitive conditions for the possibility of discourse ethics are presuppositions of argumentation. Demonstrating the impossibility of circumventing the argumentative situation therefore comes down only to recognizing that what is *implicit* in the act of argumentation is always and forever included and, unlike any other schemes of definitive justification (deductive, inductive, or abductive),[4] does not require approval of any external content. It is due to this that the procedure that legitimizes discourse ethics is a strictly reflexive, non-regressive procedure, and, in this sense, absolutely definitive.[5]

Transcendental-pragmatic justification of the theoretical project of ethics, consolidating within it the principle of co-responsibility as the superior ethical principle, as well as diagnosing the fundamental threats to which discursive rationality is exposed and the real communication community dependent on it in the face of the special power that communicative aggression has gained in the megamedia space, all provide a solid basis in order to postulate the need to construct a concept that would refer to the classical theories of mass communication and the public responsibility of the media projects. This concept could provide a basis for designing a model of public co-responsibility in relation to reality of megamedia. Such a project would have to, first of all, be indisputably a normative project. Second, it would have to be a project deriving its entire structure from the ethical principle of co-responsibility. Furthermore, it would be absolutely necessary to adapt it to the reality of the megamedia world, which would oblige to carefully cover all the aspects characteristic of megamedia communication in normative procedures. Finally, it would also have to be an essentially critical project, within a multifold (philosophical and non-philosophical) understanding of criticism. One of its particularly important tasks would be to develop the critical tools that would make it possible to expose the threats to which our rationality is and may be exposed in the context of megamedia aggression phenomena.

Of all these expectations of the theory of megamedia communication, the most questionable is that of its normative and, in part, of its critical nature. At the same time, the findings and resolutions in this regard, as well as the defense of normative and critical profiling of such a theory, are other important tasks that could be dealt with in a particularly valuable way by communication philosophy shaped in the TP perspective. These are subsequent tasks, without the fulfillment of which the chances of real and effective resistance to media aggression will not be possible.

## Notes

1 In TP, it is proposed to distinguish the so-called part A of ethics from its part B, which, to put it briefly, is a separation of the level of normative discourse ethics (along with its abstract and general—imperatively formulated—norms) and the level of co-responsibility ethics—justifying material, historically related norms of activity). Part B of ethics is therefore also normative ethics, but it obtains its own legitimation within part A, which, being purely abstract and formulating pure principles of discourse, cannot by itself serve to legitimize material principles.
2 See Endnotes 1 and 2 in Chapter 6.
3 It is important not to confuse questioning the norms of argumentation—as the first sentence of the cited conjunction says—with the commitment and necessity to problematize the claims made in immediate argumentation.
4 Within such procedures, the vast majority of analyses remain more or less directly related to the problem of ethics and ethical norms. And all these procedures use, as supreme, the principle of propositional non-contradiction, while in the strict reflection procedure, the superior role is assigned to the principle of performative non-self-contradiction.
5 Its legitimacy cannot be justified empirically or through reconstruction proceedings. In the latter case, the main moral principles can, in fact, acquire the status of a theoretical axiom at best.

# 9 Toward a Normative Media Theory

To recapitulate, the new face of media communication, its megamedia face, has not caused any special qualitative changes in terms of the forms of communicative aggression invariably accompanying human speech. However, it has caused its consequences to spread in a completely new way. In particular, it has caused the effects of megamedia aggression to reach the very foundations of the communication relation, directly threatening the structural foundations of discursive rationality and its determinants to the highest degree. Thus, it has threatened the destruction of the conditions for the possibility of communication cooperation and the real communication community.

The unquestionable requirement resulting from this situation—extremely important but not the only one—is the development of a new coherent theory of media communication, within which it would be possible to conceptualize the megamedia space, with particular emphasis on the diagnosis of threats and the (as we have seen, numerous) negative phenomena associated with it. Media aggression is a phenomenon of particularly dangerous consequences that—as shown by transcendental-pragmatic analyses—absolutely entails the construction not only of a coherent theory of media communication but also of a new model of social co-responsibility embedded in it. On the part of communication philosophy, a solid theoretical ground has been prepared through the construction and justification of the project of discourse ethics and the act of deriving from it the principle of co-responsibility as the main ethical principle. These steps must be absolutely completed by resolving the question of how the normativity and criticism of such a concept are possible. For both, the general philosophical perspective developed by TP and the detailed diagnoses of megamedia communication—and especially of aggression flooding it—leave no doubt that the concept of the megamedia sphere required today has to be normative and critical. All the indications reveal that normativity may be inherited directly from the ethical principle upon which it is founded (Apel 1973), whereas criticism may find legitimation in the very structure of communicative *a priori* (Sierocka 2003).

A dispute on whether and how normativity is possible—and also whether it is essential and in any way required—has already been held at many levels. It was applied both to general philosophical theories and to the ethics projects, as well as to concepts concerning the sphere of media communication—to be limited only to the problem areas that fall within the competences of communication philosophy. While the distinction of a normative approach was made in a fairly legible and, above all, conscious (which does not mean consistent or even justified) manner in philosophy and ethics, based on media (mass) communication theory, distinctions related to normativity remained unclear. These concepts did not use general declarations, and their normative character was often revealed only due to subsequent reconstructions or collective analyses. Thus far, no research on the justification of normativity has been undertaken based on these concepts either: as a rule, these theories have not been associated with such competences at all. Normativity simply appeared in them, usually as an obvious response to the more or less severe shortcomings of the media in meeting social expectations and satisfying important social needs. This was clearly the case with the concepts outlined in the Hutchins Report and in *Four Theories of the Press* by Schramm, Siebert, and Peterson, or in Bertrand's project. However, these three constructions do not exhaust the list of normatively profiled theories of media communication. Their multiplicity and noticeable diversity prompted, for example, Denis McQuail to indicate as many as four different models, which are not too sharply separated from each other but are clearly guided by "different internal logic" (McQuail 2010). It is a set that also very well reflects the dynamics of changes in the four-part relation "individual—media—market—state." The following are distinguished here: (1) "liberal-pluralist model" or the "market model," (2) the "model of social responsibility" or "public interest," (3) the "professional model," and (4) the "model of alternative media." All these relate to mass media communication and—to a very limited extent—fit into the reality of megamedia. The "alternative media model" may seem closest to them, but the actual theoretical references turn out to be scarcely possible. This is because there is a clear "rejection of universal rationality" within this model, whereas the global, total, and universal range of megamedia communication absolutely forces such a range of rationality. Furthermore, the theory referred to it should—precisely as a normative theory—definitely impose such universality (certainly only in the argumentative mode).

However, as has already been suggested, the superior problem is the question of the extent to which a normative theory is possible at all; this indirectly allows for the consideration of how and to what extent this may be necessary. On the basis of TP, this question is formulated as such and is set in this theoretical context, which is also a question about its own legitimation. The issue of founding a normative theory coincides in a special way with the issue of the legitimation of the theoretical question regarding the possibility of a normative theory. Such a situation was conceptualized by Apel in the context of a very interesting and originally developed problem regarding the self-matching (*Selbsteinholung*) of historical and social sciences (Apel 1996).

Nonetheless, the starting point is a dispute over normativity. Such a dispute of a fundamental nature requires resolutions on essential issues that may be ontological and axiological and, above all, epistemological. As such, this dispute sharply polarizes theoretical opinions and takes place in the field of philosophy but naturally transfers to other social sciences (including the theory of media communication). In every case, the polemic concerning it is connected with the most serious theoretical, ideological, or worldview resolutions.

The axis of this dispute is determined by the distinction of "fact–value" (or to express it in a more traditional language: "existence–responsibility"). Essentially, all its aspects come down to the arrangements of the relations among the elements of these distinctions. However, as in the case of other abovementioned contradictory pairs, which have "organized" the European philosophical debate (or, in fact, the entire European thinking) since deep antiquity, the most conclusive question in this case is how justified this actual distinction is. Its undermining (and argumentation leading to it) turned out to be a chance to settle a dispute and finally legitimize the possibility of an objective normative theory. This was made possible only after noticing the linguistic and communicative foundations of knowledge. It was no coincidence that the first inspirations in this direction were to be read (Apel 1976) in the texts of John Searle, a philosopher whose resolutions in the field of epistemology or theory of knowledge were shaped by the post-Austinian and post-Wittgensteinian philosophies of colloquial language and his own concept of speech acts. This conceptualization of language as a sphere of cooperative activities prompted Searle to recognize just how inadequate the so-called criticism of "naturalistic fallacy" is.

This simply means recognizing the inadequacy of the separation between facts and values, between descriptive statements and normative statements (evaluative), as analytic philosophy reformulated the issue, or—in a different approach—between the criteria for applying an evaluative statement and its meaning (Apel 1976).

However, on the one hand, from the perspective of TP, it can be clearly seen that Searle's philosophy, by constructing another level of reflection on the "fact–value" opposition (and thus by building a metacriticism of the criticism of "naturalistic fallacy"), discovers the correct theoretical "path" leading beyond the "fact–value" dilemma. On the other hand, it does not take the "path" and basically loses the chance to legitimize normativity. This opinion is worthy of attention, as it sheds light on a situation typical not only of Searle's concept but also of all contemporary theoretical trends that have taken up the issue of the possibility of a normative theory (not only ethical).

What built this groundbreaking path for Searle was the general line on which he conducted his metacriticism. In the most general plan, he pointed out that attempts to embed the traditional metaphysical distinction between fact and value in linguistic matter are groundless. This is how, to put it simply, analytic metaethics conducted its criticism of "naturalistic fallacy." On the one hand, assuming that it is impossible to derive **evaluative** judgments from descriptive judgments and that, on the other hand, only the content that is normatively neutral, "objective," and free from evaluation can have scientific qualification, it stated that establishing a legitimate and normative ethical theory is impossible. Meanwhile, as revealed by Searle's illocutionary theory of speech acts, the indissolubility and inseparability of both dimensions (facts and values) result from the specific structure of these acts. As Searle puts it, "speaking a language is everywhere saturated with the facts of making commitments, accepting commitments, presenting convincing reasoning, and so on." The decisive factor, according to him, is that speaking "consists in performing speech activities in accordance with the rules, and it is impossible to separate these speech acts from obligations that make up a significant part of them" (Searle 1969; Apel 1976). Searle considers this belief to be the "main motive" of his speech act theory.

In this general line, according to which Searle conducted his metacriticism, was the first outline of the conditions for the illocutionary force of speech acts, that is, the theoretical idea, which was then translated by Jürgen Habermas into the famous concept of validity claims (Searle 1975; Habermas 1981). It was this construction that constituted a particular feature of this completely new approach, proposed by Searle, which became extremely significant for many issues and not just for the problem of normativity. For most of them, it was definitely a revealing approach, including efforts to find a valid and credible normative theory, for which it has set a completely new theoretical perspective (especially close to the transcendental-pragmatic concept).

What closed the way for Searle's philosophy to establish a legitimate normative theory is—in the opinion of TP—that it understands and leads the analysis of speech acts as reflection on universal rules which in all describable linguistic institutions are—as Searle himself says—"conventionally realized." The reduction of these analyses to the description of "institutional facts" constitutes a significant **inconsistency** into which Searle's analyses fall and which, from the position of transcendental pragmatics, is considered the reason why they are unsuitable for executing the definitive resolution of the problem of normative ethics. This weakness is puzzling because the theoretical perspective and the tools provided by Searle's illocutionary concept of speech acts are the ones that permit the analysis of speech acts in such a way that these analyses transform into reflection on rules that no longer have the character of contingent, describable institutional facts, but are norms of activities that have to always and forever be accepted *a priori* if it is to be possible to describe the facts or even to communicate in a language at all (Apel 1976).

These norms, whether as a transcendental (necessary and *a priori*) framework for an argumentative discourse or as rules related to specific and detailed obligations, cannot achieve legitimation by deducing duties from the existence of institutional linguistic facts or by deducing normative statements from empirical descriptions of facts. Inductive or abductive procedures are equally useless to them. Critics of the idea of definitive justification are right: neither of these ways can guarantee an absolute result. However, this does not mean that it is unattainable—that it is impossible to legitimize norms and, consequently, legitimize normative ethics. The essence of the matter, however, is to trust in the intellectual procedures of a completely different nature and not to seek new resolutions (whether positive or critical) based on a deductive procedure. The only procedure that can be reasonably involved in the search for the legitimation of norms is the procedure referred to as close reflection, which is in accordance with the previously mentioned TP findings. In this procedure (modeled on not entirely consistent argumentation strategies developed by Descartes, Kant, or Fichte), it is primarily about reflection, which—as Leibniz postulated for the first time with a different intention—primarily makes use of itself. In other words, it relates first to itself; then, through this self-relevance, it can—in a special case—recognize the definitive basis of knowledge. As we have seen, based on communication philosophy, this procedure leads to the presentation of what has always and forever been included in the structure of the communication act as its *a priori* condition for such a possibility. Furthermore, in view of the communicative constitution of knowledge and the communicative nature of all human cooperation, the fundamental determinants of knowledge—the proper basis—are revealed. This basis is the impossibility of circumventing the argumentative situation and the immanent presence of the norms of argumentative discourse in the structure of the communication relation. Thus, the legitimacy and credibility of normative ethics are ultimately guaranteed due to the formal conditions for the communication act, which also determine the content of its moral implications. Revealing these dependencies and proving the legitimacy of normative theory is tantamount to recognizing the indispensable embedding of every social theory in the project of discourse ethics, while simultaneously demonstrating the *a priori* necessity of the norms constituting these ethics.

In other words, indicating that the argumentative situation is uncircumventable and that we are inalienably bound by the norms of argumentative discourse—under the threat of performative self-contradiction, that is, breaking out of the framework of discursive rationality—is the foundation for constructing normative social theories. This is the right basis for building a normative theory of media communication. Moreover, this is the basic determinant of the direction that such a theory should take, as well as a guarantor of the highest quality of its reliability, accuracy, and intellectual openness. At the same time, it becomes a source of well-motivated hope for its effectiveness, which has a value that cannot be overestimated, especially in the context of the current problems we face due to megamedia aggression.

Obviously, the background offered by communication philosophy to the postulated theory of megamedia communication (i.e., the construction of the project of discourse ethics, its legitimation and the derivation of the principle of co-responsibility as the superior moral obligation, and the legitimation of the normativity of the ethical theory) is only the beginning. It is only the preparation of the theoretical background upon which the theory of megamedia communication should be based. Nonetheless, it is the background that is absolutely compulsory, especially if we expect an extensive model of social co-responsibility from this theory and if we hope to use it as an effective form of resistance against media aggression.

Given that we are talking about efficiency, within this context, it is indispensable to focus—even briefly—on an issue that is particularly strongly related to it. The effectiveness of a social theory, although measured by many determinants, is always largely determined by its inherent critical force. Although this thesis is not indisputable, the opinion that criticism is the highest measure of this effectiveness can even be defended. Nonetheless, the long history of philosophical (and non-philosophical) search for the right formula of criticism, its most effective tools, and the appropriate criteria or arguments legitimizing it definitely prove the indispensable need to have these critical tools within a social theory. Concepts related to the space of media communication absolutely require such tools as well.

Ultimately, the construction of critical projects has always been the responsibility of philosophy, which has typically performed this task scrupulously. If we wanted to collect and briefly summarize the effects of these efforts, it should be noted that, first of all, as the result of these efforts, three different types of intellectual attitudes were shaped on the basis of philosophy: ironic, skeptical, and critical attitudes (Sierocka 2003). In some respects, they are indistinguishable from one another, yet definitely separate. Each of them has been developed in philosophy since deep antiquity, and it is precisely criticism that needed the longest time to obtain the full variety and depth of its shape. Second, we can talk about many models of critique, consciously shaped and intensively used by philosophy both on its own ground and in other disciplines (including the theory of media communication). The typology of the models of critique—those relevant to the theory of communication in general and therefore to the theory of media communication—could be briefly presented in a simple list that differentiates its models based on the specificity of the intellectual procedures implemented. Such a summary can be presented as follows:

- **Criticism as a justifying procedure**, that is,
  - a procedure revealing the *a priori* conditions for the possibility of knowledge, and
  - a procedure based on the so-called "strict reflection."

- **Criticism as a procedure revealing infringements of the rigor of discursiveness,** that is,
  - a procedure exposing the manifestations of the erosion of discursiveness as well as the destruction of stability and rationality, and
  - the critical procedures subordinated to the principle of performative non-contradiction.
- **Criticism as a procedure revealing enslavement by the compulsion of identity**, that is,
  - a procedure exposing the delusional, totalizing, and excluding character of identity thinking, and
  - a critical procedure realized as the philosophy of non-identity exposing "thinking by models."
- **Criticism as a procedure revealing the oppressiveness of reason**, that is,
  - a procedure exposing the antinomicity and self-destructiveness of reason as well as the excluding and repressive power of knowledge, and
  - a critical procedure as archeology of knowledge and genealogy of power.
- **Criticism as an evaluation procedure** (classic shape of criticism as *ars iudicandi*), that is,
  - a procedure that discriminates due to the adopted values (e.g., due to truth), and
  - procedures subjugated to the principle of propositional non-contradiction.

Such an ordering of the models of critique is just a general one. It does not take into consideration many nuances nor does it mention many important characteristics and conclusive ideas. However, it certainly points to the types of critical procedures that have been constructed in view of the fundamental as well as the most important and difficult questions about our knowledge and rationality. At the same time, these procedures are particularly well suited to the needs of the theory, which, as postulated, faces the task of creating a model of public co-responsibility of the media as a weapon against the destructive power of megamedia aggression.

However, these procedures are used to varying degrees and are differently assessed in terms of real research practices or in purely theoretical projects. The important thing is to make the most out of the valuable critical potential that can be directly or indirectly extracted from philosophical concepts, at least those that directly declare criticism as the principal dimension of their projects. In the face of the threats with which the communication community is confronted, and above all in the face of the destructive power of megamedia aggression, this should be done in order to activate the critical tools at every possible level of research and the theory and to be fully aware of their indispensability.

In principle, there is no doubt as to the importance of those critical procedures that fit into the first of the models mentioned and thus serve to legitimize knowledge. At the same time, this is the type of procedure that is solely within the competence of philosophy, and due to close reflection that is characteristic of the transcendental perspective, philosophy considers the theoretical duty for developing the procedures of justification. This theoretical responsibility, on the one hand, has been fully overtaken by TP, constructing the foundations of the project of communication philosophy, which owes its shape to the communication theory transformation of Kantian transcendentalism. On the other hand, non-philosophical theories, which do not possess the competences of philosophy in this respect, must be able to situate their own theoretical constructions on the basis of these philosophical achievements. Given that these achievements owe their strength to the communication theory profile, such a condition must absolutely be met, especially by those social disciplines whose subject areas are related to the space of media communication.

The next three models of critique include procedures that, based on philosophy, can be used in an interesting and valuable way in almost every discipline in the field of social sciences. In fact, they should be obligatorily present there. They relate to phenomena observed in all dimensions of social reality and are characterized by an exceptional specific gravity. It is about phenomena that are classified as infringing upon the stability of socially formed rationality leading to the self-destruction of prevailing rationality. They all result in some way—as Kant once put it—from the "natural dialectic of reason" and are thus related to certain immanent mechanisms organizing our rationality. Three clearly distinguished complexes of phenomena at which criticism is directed in the subsequent models can be described in a concise form: (1) erosion of discursiveness, (2) the compulsion of identity, and (3) the power of oppressive reason. In turn, the models of critique applied to each of these complexes are to be captured in their fullest form within (1) transcendental pragmatics, (2) negative dialectic, and (3) the archeology of knowledge and genealogy of power.

Each of these concepts theoretically struggles with the most powerful issues—each trying to construct a diagnosis of the most difficult problems faced by the prevailing rationality resulting from this "natural dialectic of reason." The most fundamental levels are reached primarily by transcendental pragmatics as a theory seeking *a priori* conditions for knowledge, and its critical force comes from such a process. It reveals that permanent exposure of the communication acts to performative contradiction implies the need to relate critical procedures to the criteria of validity and the status of validity claims as well as the criteria of the validity and the status of related norms, obligations, and duties. It is also important that the critical procedures are located at two different levels, which is related to the specific approach of TP to these validity claims. The fact remains that one of four claims specified in universal pragmatics by Habermas—the claim to intersubjectively valid sense—is placed by transcendental pragmatics at a deeper level than the other claims, thus considering it superior to the others. "As *semanticos logos* of natural language, it is, due to the dual performative-propositional structure of language, a condition for the possibility of these three other universal validity claims" (Apel 1986), that is, claims related to sincerity, truth, and normative rightness (Apel 1986). Thus, the claim to intersubjectively valid sense is perceived by TP as the most fundamental validity claim of human *logos* (Apel 1996). This is of great importance, because the criticism postulated here is, in fact, the accurate reconstruction of Wittgenstein's project of the critique of meaning, however, embedded in the transcendental perspective. Moreover, Wittgenstein's inspirations mean that the conditions for meaningfulness revealed in a critical procedure are no longer equated here with "semantic possibility," that is, with conditions for the possibility of truth statements, as was the case in Wittgenstein's *Logical Philosophical Treatise*. According to TP, the criterion of sense is determined and legitimized by reference to the uncircumventable structure of argumentation. It comes down to a simple cliché that a linguistic communication act is meaningful, which—respecting the principle of the definitive consensus of the unlimited communication community and conforming to the normative rule of the categorical imperative—can be assessed with regard to obligations, claims, and norms brought, and thus qualified as either successful or unsuccessful. In turn, the criteria of this assessment include immanent rules for the very *a priori* structure of argumentation.

Thus, the fundamental tasks that are assigned within this model to the critical analysis are (in view of constant exposure of discursive rationality to deep erosion), first, determining limits (and thus the conditions for possibility) of interpersonally valid meaning, and second, constant theoretical and practical willingness to problematize claims and duties, which determine this rationality in terms of their validity and status. These are tasks that must be shared with philosophy by every theory related to the area of communication. For the postulated theory of megamedia communication, taking over these tasks and their specific "popularizing" is definitely a predominant duty.

Although the perspectives of apriorism and transcendentalism are strange to the two other models of critique listed, they also reach with their uncompromising criticism the fundamental dimensions of rationality. Both in the negative dialectic of Theodor Adorno and in the genealogy constructed by Michael Foucault and even earlier in the archeology of knowledge, philosophical inquiries take the form of radically critical analyses that reveal deep mechanisms and coherent, "solidified" categorial structures that condition rationality. These are the mechanisms and structures that are equally responsible for its creativity, knowledge-creating potential, power of enslavement, and power of unreason. Both philosophers—admittedly immersed in the same sociocultural reality and drawing theoretical inspiration from the works of the greatest "masters of suspicions" (Nietzsche, Marx, and Freud)—conducted their critical thoughts completely independently of one another, and yet (in many of the most important aspects) they spoke as if with one philosophical voice. This theoretical relationship could be broken down into many different aspects, but the most important thing is that both concepts develop a very subtle model of critique—one in which consistent and uncompromising radicalism of criticism does not generate a nihilistic, irrational, or skeptical attitude (in its classic understanding). Criticism of thinking (as it is called in negative dialectic) and of reason (as genealogy puts it)[1] is the penetration of rationality that reveals the subversive dialectic that Kant diagnosed in his transcendental research. Oppressiveness, self-destruction, unreason, ideologicality, and dogmaticity are "shortcomings" that are fatal to rationality—but are precisely those that (exposed by critical procedures) result from mechanisms immanent to rationality itself and which somehow constitute its indispensable "constructing material." First of all, it is this specific relation that must be considered by responsible critical analysis. The outline according to which the history of rationality develops is quite clear: its erosion is ultimately a consequence of falsehood and semblance it generates—only that it is "necessary semblance," and therefore, it can never be eliminated ultimately and radically (irretrievably). Furthermore, it is semblance that—due to the subtle and consistently critical analysis (free from both dogmatism and skepticism)—can and should be revealed. However, that does not mean that it is possible to eliminate the mechanisms responsible for its formation.

The fact that critical analyses carried out in both models restrictively move away and question all the external criteria and instances on which they would be supported and which would provide them with the necessary sanctions is specific and extremely important to them. It is a feature of critical thinking straight from Kantian and Nietzschean efforts to achieve consistent and coherent design of criticism—a feature that is strongly supported by the concept of discursiveness and is extremely difficult to maintain. Nevertheless, it is unconditionally necessary, as it ultimately determines the real critical potential of the developed thought.

These two key features undoubtedly attest to the significant (and very inspiring) theoretical relationship of negative dialectic and genealogy. Nonetheless, the content that makes them distinct and unique is equally valuable and very interesting. This content appears at the level of a natural question regarding the sources and causes of the diagnosed "real semblance"—these are questions about the real causes of threats to which rationality is permanently exposed. In response to these questions, these two concepts seem to simply complement each other, accurately formulating complementary diagnoses, which should definitely constitute the important models for critical social concepts, including those that deal with the complicated matter of media communication.

In negative dialectic, the search for the sources of semblance, falsehood, and the illusory content that weighs heavily on rationality leads to a diagnosis of the power of identity thinking as an integral intellectual formation that, unknowingly subjected to the "compulsion of identity," is involved and enslaved by all those constructions that encapsulate the "compulsion of identity," ultimately laying the foundations of our rationality. The contents of identity thinking are shaped not only by the principle of identity, as a subsumption of what is individual, different, and distinct under the general notion, but also by a solid, coherent, and conceptual structure in which the most strongly established concepts are the category of unity, the category of what is first, the source, the primary, the category of the whole, the system, the unchanging, the necessary, and so on. These categories, which are responsible for false distinctions, excluding patterns, and repressive hierarchies as much as the identity principle, owe their strength to the fact that they are based on purely formal properties and principles of conceptual thinking. Moreover, they gain significant strength due to the fact that the fundamental outline organizing identity thinking (adopted as unknowingly and without reflection as the disclosed categorial structure and the principle of identity itself) are rigid dual oppositions that organize all areas of prevailing rationality.

In resistance against the indivisible domination of the principle of identity and the intellectual formation supported on it, negative dialectic, on the one hand, gives itself the shape of an anti-identity thought, which determines both a specific model of critique and the intellectual standards necessary for implementation, thereby immunizing—as Adorno used to say—to the compulsion of identity. Given the notion that "to think is to identify" (Adorno 1966), that is, to reduce the multiplicity of object configurations to one class of abstraction, thus the real result of anti-identity criticism can, at most, be immunization, that is, immunization to the compelling force of the compulsion of identity, to the traps of dual distinctions, and to the falsehood of deceptive categorial structures. Although these results are never fully achieved, this process is the only way to reveal the real semblance and to actively resist it intellectually. At the same time, it is the highest value that Adorno's negative dialectic brings to the history of critical thought.

On the other hand, critical analyses developed on the basis of Michel Foucault's philosophy are clearly stretched along two lines of tension, and they mainly owe their extraordinary strength to them (Foucault 1966, 1975b). First, they penetrate in detail the complex and multithreaded relations of knowledge and power, and, second, with great insight (and originality), they reconstruct processes that take place on the border between reason and unreason. "Knowledge and power" and "reason and unreason" are—despite transformations and visible turns experienced by Foucault's philosophy—the subjects that invariably organize the whole of his critical project. All the threads relevant to this model of critique are developed on their basis. This notion is true regardless of whether its analyses concern the illusory nature of traditional metaphysical categories and total falsehoods arising from them, whether they refer to the current "collective fiction" generated by dominant knowledge, or whether they are caused by the intention of exposing the tyranny of global discourses and their complex relationships with power.

Capturing these situations in the nuanced critical analysis, as proposed by Foucault, allows one to see a—rarely noticeable—confusing game in which power and knowledge, reason, and what is beyond reason constantly interpenetrate one another. As if incidentally, they also allow capturing the subtleties and ambiguities that a critical thought deals with, if it is to remain within the framework set for it, thus protecting it from dogmatism, nihilism, simplifications, and ordinary falsehoods. Both these aspects are essential for shaping a critical profile that should be incorporated into the theory of megamedia communication and is necessary in reliably extracting and interpreting all the features and tendencies that determine the condition for our rationality in the megamedia space.

The archeology of knowledge and genealogy of power are those specific shapes of critical thinking which—as effectively as it is in the case of negative dialectic—even masterfully teach us to see the extent to which the power of oppressiveness of reason closely correlates with its efficiency in generating false distinctions, arbitrary setting of boundaries of reason, creating apparent identities, and performing self-appointed supervision. They commit to carefully tracking down the ways by which the compulsion of identity and the demands of power trigger the precise mechanisms of social exclusion, discrimination, and alienation. At the same time, they oblige us to be extremely careful with regard to even the smallest manifestations of enslaving and subjugating everything that is different, strange, or separate.

The importance of this type of message cannot be overestimated, especially in view of such an urgent concern as the need to gain critical insights into the power of megamedia aggression, which destroys the fundamental dimensions of rationality. To put it simply, it is impossible to construct a valuable theory concerning the space of megamedia communication without the use of the critical tools developed by philosophers within the presented models of critique and the one that appeared last on the proposed list, and which—in the version of moderate fallibilism—quite naturally constitutes the base of any reasonable theoretical proposition. The creators of each of these critical models could recommend themselves—and therefore their projects—with a phrase with which Michel Foucault concluded one of his interviews: "I am a tool dealer, recipe maker, goal indicator, cartographer, plan maker, arms dealer (...)" (Foucault 1975a, in Banasiak 1988). Such professionals can undoubtedly be trusted!

## Note

1 The notion of reason was also crucial for the theoreticians of the Frankfurt School, including Max Horkheimer (primarily in the concept of instrumental reason), Herbert Marcuse, and Walter Benjamin.

# Conclusion
## To Protect οἶκος

Several years ago, Craig (2008) distinguished seven different traditions of communication research: rhetorical, semiotic, phenomenological, cybernetic, sociopsychological, sociocultural, and critical. Behind this multiplicity of traditions lies a variety of disciplines examining communication issues. These include completely new ones and certain subdisciplines (e.g., ethnolinguistics, sociolinguistics, or psycholinguistics), shaped just with the "discovery" of the communication space, which—apart from rhetoric—neither empirical disciplines nor philosophy actually reached for many centuries. The current multitude of research and reflection on communication can quickly compensate for this centuries-old "negligence" of communication practices. However, in order for the "map" of these theoretical undertakings to be complete, and for their abundance and diversity to be included in a coherent construct, the list proposed by Craig must be accomplished, and a transcendental-pragmatic perspective ought to be integrated among these traditions. The necessity and legitimacy of this completion result primarily from the rank of communication philosophy, shaped on its basis, for research and theories related to communication, which, I hope, is confirmed by the reconstructions and analyses presented.

From the point of view of the superior problem stated here, that is, the problem of megamedia aggression, this perspective seems to be crucial. Its special rank results from the fact that the comprehensive diagnosis of aggression observed in the media space, which it formulates, is also the diagnosis of the condition of the communication community and rationality that establishes its coherence. This coupling is indisputably crucial. First of all, it makes it possible to clearly notice the extent to which the presence of aggression in the megamedia space constitutes a direct and extremely serious threat to the communication community. At the same time, it allows us to understand that this threat is a direct consequence of the destruction of the foundations of rationality made by aggression. Thus, this coupling enables a reliable assessment of the condition of our rationality and equips us with the necessary tools to legitimize the principle of co-responsibility as the highest ethical principle upon which the functioning of a real communication community has to be based.

The diagnosis presented by communication philosophy carries an extremely important message: it makes us aware that the meticulous (always maintained in the mode of argumentative discourse) concern for rationality, including—above all—its radical protection against megamedia aggression, is, in fact, the foundation of protection for our real home, our οἶκος. If it could be expressed in a somewhat sublime tone, it would be that it is our inalienable **ecological duty.**

This is because our household, that is, our natural environment, is not only a biosystem—it is also a sociosystem bonded only by the power of the rationality we construct. It is precisely its shortcomings—the cracks and "turbulences," weaknesses, and falsehood—that are the most powerful source of mutilations suffered by the communication community and which destroy our οἶκος. And the power of aggression observed in the megamedia space, which is destructive for rationality, demands extraordinary consideration, although it is still difficult to perceive and requires a coherent conceptualization. Hence, our ecological duty is absolutely imperative. The decisive thing here is that acts of media-mediated aggression mutilate the communication community deeply and irrevocably in a way that **violates the inalienable conditions of its existence**, thereby destroying the rationality that establishes it. They threaten an impending disaster comparable to what environmentalists are warning against nowadays due to the devastation of the natural environment.

It is absolutely necessary to understand that both threats are of the same rank and that both require our unconditional intervention. We are becoming increasingly aware of the effects produced by the devastation of our planet. However, the effects of the mutilation of the communication community have not yet penetrated our consciousness. It is time for us to understand these effects. It is time for us to prevent them.

# References

Adorno, Theodor W., and Max Horkheimer. 1947. *Dialektik der Aufklärung: Philosophische Fragmente*. Amsterdam: Querido.
Adorno, W. Theodor. 1966. *Gesammelte Schriften*, B.6. Frankfurt am Main: Suhrkamp.
Anderson, Craig A., William E. Deuser, and Kristina DeNeve. 1995. "Hot temperatures, hostile affect, hostile cognition, and arousal: Tests of the general model of affective aggression." *Personality and Social Psychology Bulletin*, 21: 434–448.
Apel, Karl-Otto. 1973. *Transformation der Philosophie*, v. 1–2. Frankfurt am Main: Suhrkamp.
Apel, Karl-Otto. 1976. "Sprechakttheorie und transzendentale Sprachpragmatik zur Frage ethischer Normen." In *Sprachpragmatik und Philosophie*, edited by Karl-Otto Apel. Frankfurt am Main: Suhrkamp, 106–173.
Apel, Karl Otto. 1978. "Transformation der Transzendentalphilosophie. Versuch einer retrospektiven Zwischenbilanz." *"Philosophische Selbstbetrachtungen,"* t. IV, Bern: Peter Lang, 7–23.
Apel, Karl-Otto. 1986. "Logosauszeichnung der menschlichen Sprache. Die philosophische Tragweite der Sprachtheorie." In *Perspektiven auf Sprache. Interdisziplinäre Beiträge zum Gedenken an Hans Hörmann*, edited by Hans-Georg Bosshard. Berlin/New York: De Gruyter, 45–87.
Apel, Karl-Otto. 1996. "Die Vernunftfunktion der kommunikativen Rationalität. Zum Verhältnis von konsensualkommunikativer Rationalität, strategischer Rationalität und Systemrationalität." In *Die eine Vernunft und die vielen Rationalitäten*, edited by Karl-Otto Apel, and Matthias Kettner. Frankfurt am Main: Suhrkamp, 17–41.
Austin, L. John. 1976. *How to Do Things with Words*. Oxford: Oxford University Press.
Banasiak, Bogdan. 1988. "Michel Foucault—mikrofizyka władzy." *Literatura na Świecie*, 6: 330–338.
Bandura, Albert. 1973. *Aggression: A Social Learning Analysis*. Edgewood Cliffs, NJ: Prentice-Hall.
Baran, Stanley J., and Davis Dennis K. 2002. *Mass Communication Theory: Foundations, Ferment, and Future*. Belmont, CA: Wadsworth.

Baron-Cohen, Simon. 2011. *The Science of Evil: On Empathy and the Origins of Cruelty*. London: Basic Books, Penguin.
Battelle, John. 2005. *The Search: How Google and Its Rivals Rewrote the Rules of Business and Transformed Our Culture*. New York: Portfolio.
Bauer, Joachim. 2011. *Schmerzgrenze. Vom Ursprung alltäglicher und globaler Gewalt*. München: Karl Blessing Verlag.
Bauman, Sheri. 2019. Political Cyberbullying: Perpetrators and Targets of a New Digital Aggression. Santa Barbara: ABC-CLIO, LLC.
Berkowitz, Leonard. 1973. *Aggression: A Social Psychological Analysis*. New York: McGraw-Hill.
Berners-Lee, Tim. 1999. *Weaving the Web*. San Francisco, CA: Harper.
Bernstein, Michael S., Andrés Monroy-Hernández, Drew Harry, Paul André, Katrina Panovich, and Greg Vargas. 2011. "4chan and /b/: An analysis of anonymity and ephemerality in a large online community." In *Proceedings of the Fifth International AAAI Conference on Weblogs and Social Media*. Barcelona: AAAI Press. https://www.researchgate.net/publication/221297869_4chan_and_b_An_Analysis_of_Anonymity_and_Ephemerality_in_a_Large_Online_Community
Bertrand, Claude-Jean. 1997. *La déontologie des médias*. Paris: PUF.
Bolton, Robert. 1979. *People Skills: How to Assert Yourself, Listen to Others, and Resolve Conflicts*. New York: Simon & Schuster.
Böhler, Dietrich. 1985. *Rekonstruktive Pragmatik: Von der Bewußtseinsphilosophie zur Kommunikationsreflexion—Neubegründung der praktischen Wissenschaften und Philosophie*. Frankfurt am Main: Suhrkamp.
Böhler, Dietrich. 1994. *Ethik für Zukunft. Im Diskurs mit Hans Jonas*. München: C. H. Beck.
Bruner, Jerome. 1986. *Actual Minds, Possible Worlds*. Cambridge, MA: Harvard University Press.
Buber, Martin. 2008. *Ich und Du*. Stuttgart: Reclam.
Butler, Judith. 1997. *Excitable Speech: A Politics of the Performative*. New York: Routledge.
Castells, Manuel. 1998. *End of Millennium, The Information Age: Economy, Society and Culture*, Vol. III. Cambridge, MA, Oxford: Blackwell.
Castells, Manuel. 2001. *The Internet Galaxy: Reflections on the Internet, Business, and Society*. Oxford: Oxford University Press.
Chang, Briankle G., and Garnet C. Butchart (eds.). 2012. *Philosophy of Communication*. Cambridge, MA: MIT Press.
Cheng, Justin, Michael Bernstein, Cristian Danescu-Niculescu-Mizil, and Jure Leskovec. 2017. "Anyone can become a troll: Causes of trolling behavior in online discussions." CSCW '17: Proceedings of the 2017 ACM Conference on Computer Supported Cooperative Work and Social Computing February 2017, 1217–1230. doi:10.1145/2998181.2998213
Christopherson, Kimberly. 2007. "The positive and negative implications of anonymity in Internet social interactions: "On the internet, nobody knows you're a dog."" *Computers in Human Behavior*, 23: 3038–3056.

https://www.researchgate.net/publication/222428988_The_positive_and_negative_implications_of_anonymity_in_Internet_social_interactions_On_the_Internet_Nobody_Knows_You%27re_a_Dog

Cicchirillo, Vincent, Jay Hmielowski, and Myiah Hutchens. 2015. "The mainstreaming of verbally aggressive online political behaviors." *Cyberpsychology, Behavior, and Social Networking*, 18(5): 253–259.Commission on Freedom of the Press. 1947. *A Free and Responsible Press: A General Report on Mass Communication: Newspapers, Radio, Motion Pictures*, xii, 138. Chicago, IL: University of Chicago Press.

Cook, Melissa, and Annette M. Holba (eds.). 2008. *Philosophies of Communication: Implications for Everyday Experience*. New York: Peter Lang.

Cooper, Al (ed.). 2002. *Sex and the Internet: A Guidebook for Clinicians*. New York: Brunner-Routledge.

Craig, Robert T. 2008. "Communication as a field and discipline." In *The International Encyclopedia of Communication*, edited by Wolfgang Donsbach. Oxford and Malden, MA: Blackwell Publishing, 675–688.

Crawford, Matthew. 2015. *The World beyond Your Head: On Becoming an Individual in an Age of Distraction*. New York: Farrar, Straus & Giroux.

Diener, Ed, Rob Lusk, Darlene DeFour, and Robert Flax. 1980. "Deindividuation: Effects of group size, density, number of observers, and group member similarity on self-consciousness and disinhibited behavior." *Journal of Personality and Social Psychology*, 39, 449–459.

Dollard, John, Leonard Doob, Neal Miller, Orval Hobart Mowrer, and Sears Robert. 1939. *Frustration and Aggression*. New Haven, CT: Yale University Press.

Dunbar, Robin, and Susanne Shultz. 2007. "Evolution in the social brain." *Science*, 317(5843): 1344–1347. Bibcode:2007Sci...317.1344D. doi:10.1126/science.1145463. PMID 17823343

Eliot, Thomas S. 1934. *Choruses from "The Rock."* Edited by Peter Y. Chou, WisdomPortal.com.

Erikson, Erik. 1950. *Childhood and Society*. New York: W. W. Norton & Company.

Ferguson, Christopher J., Stephanie M. Rueda, Amanda M. Cruz, Diana E. Ferguson, Stacey Fritz, and Shawn M. Smith. 2008. "Violent video games and aggression: Causal relationship or byproduct of family violence and intrinsic violence motivation?" *Criminal Justice and Behavior*, 311–332. https://www.webcitation.org/63PLhgBmk?url=http://www.tamiu.edu/~cferguson/CJBGames.pdf

Fidler, Roger. 1997. *Mediamorphosis: Understanding the New Media*. Thousand Oaks, CA: Pine Forge Press.

Fisk, Nathan. 2009. *Understanding Online Piracy: The Truth about Illegal File Sharing*. Santa Barbara, CA: ABC-CLIO.

Foucault, Michel. 1966. *Les mots et les choses: Une archéologie des sciences humaines*. Paris: Gallimard.

Foucault, Michel. 1975a. "Sur la sellette" (entretien avec J.-L. Ezine), Les Nouvelles littéraires, no 2477, 17–23 mars 1975, p. 3. Dits Ecrits tome II texte n° 152. http://1libertaire.free.fr/MFoucault125.html

Foucault, Michel. 1975b. *Surveiller et punir. La naissance de la prison.* Paris: Gallimard.

Frankl, Viktor E. 1985. *Das Leiden am sinnlosen Leben.* Freiburg–Basel–Wien: Verlag Herder.

Freud, Sigmund. 1922. *Beyond the Pleasure Principle.* Translated by Caroline Jane Mary Hubback. London, Vienna: The International Psycho-Analytical Press.

Fromm, Erich. 1973. *The Anatomy of Human Destructiveness.* London: Jonathan Cape.

Fukuyama, Francis. 1995. *Trust.* New York: The Free Press.

Gadamer, Hans-Georg. 1960. *Wahrheit und Methode: Grundzüge einer philosophischen Hermeneutik.* Tübingen: J. C. B. Mohr (Paul Siebeck).

Gerald, Edward. 1963. *The Social Responsibility of the Press.* Minneapolis, MN: University of Minnesota Press.

Giddens, Anthony. 1991. Modernity and Self-Identity. Self and Society in the Late Modern Age. Redwood City, CA: Stanford University Press.

Goban-Klas, Tomasz. 2002. *Media i komunikowanie masowe. Teorie i analizy prasy, radia, telewizji i Internetu.* Warszawa: PWN.

Gouldner, Alvin. 1960. "The norm of reciprocity: A preliminary statement." *American Sociological Review*, 25(2): 161–178. https://www.jstor.org/stable/2092623

Grice, Paul. 1975. "Logic and conversation". In *Speech Acts, Syntax and Semantics*, edited by P. Cole and J. Morgan. New York: Academic Press, 31–58.

Habermas, Jürgen. 1981. *Theorie des kommunikativen Handelns.* Volume 1: *Handlungsrationalität und gesellschaftliche Rationalisierung.* Volume 2: *Zur Kritik der funktionalistischen Vernunft.* Frankfurt am Main: Suhrkamp.

Hardin, Russell. 2002. *Trust and Trustworthiness.* New York: Russell Sage Foundation.

Haron, Haryani, and Yusof Bt. Mohd Farahidah. 2010. "Cyber stalking: The social impact of social networking technology." In *International Conference on Education and Management Technology.* https://ieeexplore.ieee.org/document/5657665

Heirman, Wannes, and Michel Walrave. 2008. "Assessing concerns and issues about the mediation of technology in cyberbullying." *Cyberpsychology: Journal of Psychosocial Research on Cyberspace*, 2(2), article 1. http://www.cyberpsychology.eu/view.php?cisloclanku=2008111401&article=1

Hill, Kim, Hurtado Magdalena. 2012. "Human reproductive assistance". *Nature,* 483: 160–161. https://www.nature.com/articles/483160a?proof=t

Hobbes, Thomas. 1651. *Leviathan or the Matter, Forme and Power of a Commonwealth Ecclesiasticall and Civil.* London: printed for Andrew Crooke, at the Green Dragonin St. Pauls Churchyard. https://socialsciences.mcmaster.ca/econ/ugcm/3ll3/hobbes/Leviathan.pdf

Jagatic, Tom, Nathaniel A. Johnson, Markus Jakobsson, and Filippo Menczer. 2007. "Social phishing." *Communications of the ACM*, 50(10). doi:10.1145/1290958.1290968

Jakobson, Roman. 1960. "Closing statements: linguistics and poetics." In *Style in Language*, edited by Thomas Sebeok. Cambridge MA: MIT Press, 350–377.

Joinson, Adam. 1998. "Causes and implications of disinhibited behavior on the Internet." In *Psychology and the Internet: Intrapersonal, Interpersonal, and Transpersonal Implications*, edited by Jayne Gackenbach. San Diego, CA: Academic Press, 43–60.

Jonas, Hans. 1979. *Das Prinzip Verantwortung: Versuch einer Ethik für die technologische Zivilisation*. Frankfurt am Maina/M.: Suhrkamp.

Kelly, James. 1981. „A philosophy of communication." *Communicatio Socialis*, 14(3): 223–231. www.communicatio-socialis.de

Kowalski, Robin M., Susan P. Limber, and Patricia W. Agatston. 2012. *Cyberbullying*. Hoboken, NJ: John Wiley & Sons.

Kowalski, Robin M., Gary W. Giumetti, Micah R. Lattanner, and Amber N. Schroeder. 2014. "Bullying in the digital age: A critical review and meta-analysis of cyberbullying research among you." *Psychological Bulletin*, 140(4), 1073–1137.

Krahé, Barbara. 2013. *The Social Psychology of Aggression*. London and New York: Routledge, Taylor & Francis Group, Psychology Press.

Krumsiek, Allison. 2017. *Cyber Mobs: Destructive Online Communities*. New York: Lucent Press.

Krzysztofek, Kazimierz. 2013. "Nowe media totalne: intruz w naszych domach." In *Nowe media a praktyki komunikacyjne*, edited by Katarzyna Pokorna-Ignatowicz, Stanisław Jędrzejewski, and Joanna Bierówka. Kraków: Krakowskie Towarzystwo Edukacyjne.

Kuhlmann, Wolfgang. 1981. "Reflexive Letztbegründung: Zur These von der Unhintergehbarkeit der Argumentationssituation." *Zeitschrift für Philosophische Forschung*, 35(1): 3–26.

Kuhlmann, Wolfgang. 1985a. "Ethik und Argumentation." In *Argumente—Argumentation*, edited by Josef Kopperschmidt and Helmut Schanze. Munich, 81–95.

Kuhlmann, Wolfgang. 1985b. *Reflexive Letztbegründung. Untersuchungen zur Transzendentalpragmatik*. Freiburg/München: Verlag Karl Alber.

Kuhlmann, Wolfgang. 1987. "Prinzip Verantwortung versus Diskursethik." *Archivio di Filosofia - Etica e pragmatica*, 1–3: 89–116.

Kuhlmann, Wolfgang. 1988. "Kant und die Transzendentalpragmatik. Transzendentale Deduktion und reflexive Letztbegründung." In *Kants transzendentale Deduktion und die Möglichkeit von Transzendentalphilosophie*, edited by Forum für Philosophie Bad Homburg. Frankfurt am Main: Suhrkamp, 193–221.

Lee, Eun-Ju. 2007. "Deindividuation effects on group polarization in computer-mediated communication: The role of group identification, public-self-awareness, and perceived argument quality." *Journal of Communication*, 57(2): 385–403.

Levinson, Paul. 2009. *New New Media*. New York: Penguin Academics.
Levi-Strauss, Cloud. 1969. *The Elementary Structures of Kinship*. Boston: Beacon.
Locke, John. 1689. *Two Treatises of Government*. London: Awnsham Churchill. https://www.yorku.ca/comninel/courses/3025pdf/Locke.pdf
Lorenz, Konrad. 1966. *On Aggression*. Translated by Marjorie Kerr Wilson. With a foreword by Julian Huxley. London and New York: Routledge.
Luhmann, Niklas. 2017. *Trust and Power*. Cambridge, Oxford and Boston: Polity.
Malinowski, Bronislaw. 1922. *Argonauts of the Western Pacific: An Account of Native Enterprise and Adventure in the Archipelagos of Melanesian New Guinea*. London: Routledge & Kegan Paul.
Malinowski, Bronisław. 1923. "The problem of meaning in primitive languages." In *The Meaning of Meaning, A Study of The Influence of Language upon Thought and of The Science of Symbolism* - with Supplementary Essays by B. Malinowski and F.G. Crookschank, edited by Charles Kay Ogden, and Ivor Armstrong Richards. London: Routledge & Kegan Paul, 296–336.
Malinowski, Bronisław. 1926. *Crime and Custom in Savage Society*. New York: Harcourt, Brace & Company.
Mangion, Claude. 2011. *Philosophical Approaches to Communication*. Bristol: Intellect Books.
Martens, Ekkehard, and Herbert Schnädelbach. 1985. *Philosophie: Ein Grundkurs*. Reinbek bei Hamburg: Rowohlt Verlag.
Mauss, Marcel. 1966. *The Gift: Forms and Functions of Exchange in Archaic Societies*. Translated by Ian Gunnison. London: Cohen & West Ltd.
Mayer-Schönberger, Viktor. 2009. *Delete: The Virtue of Forgetting in the Digital Age*. Princeton, NJ: Princeton University Press.
McCombs, Maxwell. 2004. *Setting the Agenda: The Mass Media and Public Opinion*. Cambridge: Polity Press.
McQuail, Denis. 2003. *Media Accountability and Freedom of Publication*. New York: Oxford University Press.
McQuail, Denis. 2010. *McQuail's Mass Communication Theory*. (6th edition). London, Thousand Oaks, CA, New Delhi: SAGE Publications.
Mead, George H. 1934. *Mind, Self, and Society: From the Standpoint of a Social Behaviorist*, edited, with an Introduction, by Charles W. Morris, Chicago, IL: University of Chicago Press.
Milgram, Stanley. 1963. "Behavioral study of obedience." *Journal of Abnormal and Social Psychology*, 67: 371–378.
Neisser, Ulric. 1988. "Five kinds of self-knowledge." *Philosophical Psychology*, 1(1): 35–59.
Olweus, Dan. 2012. "Cyberbullying: An overrated phenomenon?" *European Journal of Developmental Psychology*, 9: 520–538.
Pinker, Steven. 2003. *The Blank Slate: The Modern Denial of Human Nature*. London: Penguin Books.

Pinker, Steven. 2011. *The Better Angels of Our Nature: Why Violence Has Declined.* New York: Viking Adult.
Plaisance, Patrick L. 2000. "The concept of media accountability reconsidered." *Journal of Mass Media Ethics*, 15(4): 257–268.
Plomin, Robert, John C. DeFries, Gerald E. McClearn, and Peter McGuffin. 2008. *Behavioral Genetics.* New York: Worth Publishers.
Pollack, Daniel, and Andrea MacIver. 2015. "Understanding sexual *grooming* in child abuse cases." *34 Child Law Practice 161.* https://heinonline.org/HOL/LandingPage?handle=hein.journals/chilawpt34&div=81&id=&page=
Postmes, Tom, and Russell Spears. 1998. "Deindividuation and antinormative behavior: A meta-analysis." *Psychological Bulletin*, 123: 238–259.
Prensky, Marc. 2001. "Digital natives, digital immigrants Part 1." *On the Horizon*, 9(5): 1–6. http://www.marcprensky.com/ writing/prensky%20-%20digital%20natives, %20digital%20immigrants%20-%20part1.pdf
Przybylski, Andrew K., Kou Murayama, Cody R. DeHaan, and Valerie Gladwell. 2013. "Motivational, emotional, and behavioral correlates of <fear of missing out>." *Computers in Human Behavior*, 29(4), 1841–1848.
Putnam, Robert. 2000. *Bowling Alone: The Collapse and Revival of American Community.* New York: Simon & Schuster.
Putnam, Robert. 2001. "Social capital: Measurement and consequences." *Canadian Journal of Policy Research*, 2(1). http://www.oecd.org/dataoecd/25/6/1825848.pdf
Pyżalski, Jacek. 2012. "From cyberbullying to electronic aggression: Typology of the phenomenon." *Emotional and Behavioural Difficulties*, 17(3–4): s. 305–317.
Pyżalski, Jacek. 2012a. *Agresja elektroniczna i cyberbullying jako nowe ryzykowne zachowania młodzieży.* Kraków: IMPULS.
Sahlins, Marshall. 1965. "On the sociology of primitive exchange." In *The Relevance of Models for Social Anthropology*, edited by Michael Banton. London: Tavistock (ASA monographs, 1), 139–236.
Schneier, Bruce. 2015. *Data and Goliath: The Hidden Battles to Collect Your Data and Control Your World.* New York: W. W. Norton & Company.
Searle, John. 1969. *Speech Acts: An Essay in the Philosophy of Language.* Cambridge: Cambridge University Press.
Searle, John. 1975. "A taxonomy of illocutionary acts." In *Minnesota Studies in the Philosophy of Science 9: Language, Mind and Knowledge*, edited by Keith Gunderson. Minneapolis, MN: University of Minnesota Press, 344–369.
Searle, John. 1995. *The Construction of Social Reality.* New York: Free Press.
"Seville Statement on Violence." UNESCO. 1986. Retrieved 12–09–2011 http://www.unesco.org/cpp/uk/declarations/seville.pdf
Siebert, Fred S., Theodore Peterson, and Wilbur Schramm. 1956. *Four Theories of the Press. The Authoritarian, Libertarian, Social Responsibility,*

*and Soviet Communist Concepts of What the Press Should Be and Do.* Urbana: University of Illinois Press.

Sierocka, Beata. 2003. Krytyka i dyskurs: o transcendentalno-pragmatycznym uprawomocnieniu krytyki filozoficznej. Kraków: Aureus.

Sierocka, Beata. 2012. "Wokół antropologii komunikacji." In *Via communicandi: Prace z antropologii komunikacji i epistemologii społecznej*, edited by Beata Sierocka. Wrocław: Atut, 163–178.

Shaughnessy, Krystelle, Miranda Fudge, and Sandra E. Byers. 2017. "An exploration of prevalence, variety, and frequency data to quantify online sexual activity experience." *Canadian Journal of Human Sexuality*, 26, 60–75.

Shepherd, Tamara, Alison Harvey, Tim Jordan, Sam Srauy, and Kate Miltner. 2015. "Histories of Hating." *Social Media + Society*, 7–12: 1–10.

Shoemaker, Pamela J., and Tim P. Vos. 2009. *Gatekeeping Theory*. New York: Routledge.

Simmel, Georg. 1992. *Soziologie. Untersuchungen über die Formen der Vergesellschaftung*. (Georg Simmel—Gesamtausgabe, Band 11). Frankfurt am Main: Suhrkamp.

Small, Gary, and Gigi Vorgan. 2008. *iBrain: Brain: Surviving the Technological Alteration of the Modern Mind*. New York: Collins Living.

Sourander, Andre, Anat Brunstein Klomek, Maria Ikonen, Jarna Lindroos, Terhi Luntamo, Merja Koskelainen, Terja Ristkari, and Hans Helenius. 2010. "Psychosocial risk factors associated with cyberbullying among adolescents." *Archives of General Psychiatry*, 67: 720–728. doi:10.1001/archgenpsychiatry.2010.79

Sparks, Colin, and John Tulloch. 2000. *Tabloid Tales: Global Debates Over Media Standards*. Lanham, MD: Rowman & Littlefield.

Sperber, Dan, and Deirdre Wilson. 2012. *Meaning and Relevance*. Cambridge: Cambridge University Press.

Suler, John. 2004. "The online disinhibition effect." *CyberPsychology & Behavior*, 7(3): 321–326.

Sztompka, Piotr. 1999. *Trust: A Sociological Theory*. Cambridge: Cambridge University Press.

Sztompka, Piotr. 2007. *Zaufanie: fundament społeczeństwa*. Kraków: Znak.

Tomasello, Michael. 1999. *The Cultural Origins of Human Cognition*. Cambridge, MA: Harvard University Press.

Tomasello, Michael. 2009. *Why We Cooperate*. Cambridge, MA: MIT Press.

Toulouse, Chris, and Luke Timothy W. (ed.). 1998. *The Politics of Cyberspace: A New Political Sciencereader*. New York: Routledge.

Urbaniak, Paweł. 2011. "Systemy odpowiedzialności mediów jako przejaw samoregulacyjnych mechanizmów kształtowania rynku medialnego." *Studia Medioznawcze*, 2: 58–69.

Uslaner, Eric. 2002. *The Moral Foundations of Trust.* Cambridge: Cambridge University Press.
Van Dijk, Jan. 2006. *The Network Society: Social Aspects of New Media.* London, Thousand Oaks, CA, New Delhi: SAGE Publications.
Warneken, Felix, and Michael Tomasello. 2009. "The roots of human altruism." *British Journal of Psychology*, 100(3): 455–471.
Willard, Nancy. 2007. "The authority and responsibility of school officials in responding to cyberbullying." *Journal of Adolescent Health*, 41: 64–65.
Wilson, Edward O. 1978. *On Human Nature.* Cambridge, MA: Harvard University Press.
Wittgenstein, Ludwig. 1969. *On Certainty.* Edited by Elizabeth Anscombe and Georg H. von Wright, translated by Paul Denis and Elizabeth Anscombe. Oxford: Basil Blackwell.
Wittgenstein, Ludwig. 1977. *Philosophische Untersuchungen.* Frankfurt am Main: Suhrkamp.
Young, Kimberly. 1998. *Caught in Net: How to Recognize the Signs of Internet Addiction: A Sure-fire Strategy for Recovery Hardcover.* Hoboken, NJ: John Wiley & Sons.
Zimbardo, Philip G. 2007. *The Lucifer Effect: Understanding How Good People Turn Evil.* New York: Penguin Random House LLC.
Zimmerman, Adam G., and Gabriel J. Ybarra. 2014. "Online aggression: The influences of anonymity and social modeling." *Psychology of Popular Media Culture*, 6. doi:10.1037/ppm0000038

# Index

ABACUS 36
abstractive fallacy 44
Adorno, Th. W. 6, 64, 67, 72, 109, 111, 115
Agatston, P. W. 119
aggression 5–17, 28–38, 49–52, 72–6, *passim*; media 30–2, 34–5, 38, 49, 72–4, 86; megamedia 32, 34, 38, 43, 49–50, 52, 56, 73, 75, 85–6, 99, 107, 112–14
Anderson, C.A. 15, 115
André, P. 116
anonymity 35–6
Apel, K.-O. 1–2, 22, 27, 43–5, 47–8, 53, 71, 93, 95, 100–3, 108, 115
argumentation 47, 49, 70–2, 76, 90–3, 96–8, 108
argumentative act 47, 92–3, 96
argumentative discourse 71–3, 94, 103–4, 114
argumentative game 47
argumentative situation 47, 70, 90–2, 96–7, 104; uncircumventable 47, 70, 91–2, 96–7, 104, 108; impossibility to circumvent of 70, 96–7, 104
Assange, J. 86–7
Austin, L. J. 22, 46, 67, 94, 101, 115

Banasiak, B. 112, 115
Bandura, A. 9, 115
Baran, S. J. 19, 30, 115
Baron-Cohen, S. 10–12, 58, 116
Battelle, J. 29, 116
Bauer, J. 9–11, 116
Bauman, S. 30, 116
Berkowitz, L. 9, 116

Berners-Lee, T. 30, 116
Bernstein, M. S. 35, 116
Bertrand, C.-J. 82–4, 100, 116
Bierówka, J. 119
Bolton, R. 36, 116
Böhler, D. 53, 95, 116
Bruner, J. 66, 116
Brunstein Klomek, A. 116
Buber, M. 54, 116
Butchart, G. C. 116
Butler, J. 30, 116
Byers, S. E. 122

Castells, M. 25, 29, 37, 116
Chang, B. G. 41, 116
Cheng, J. 29, 116
claims 24, 46–50, 53, 62–3, 65, 71, 89–94, 98, 108–9; validity claims 53, 75, 91, 103, 108; for consensus 61
Christopherson, K. 35, 116
Cicchirillo, V. 30, 117
consensus 50, 61, 71–2, 74, 91–4; definitive 48, 53, 70, 72–3, 76, 108; ideal 71, 73
Cook, M. 43, 117
Cooper, A. 29, 117
co-intentionality 27, 46, 55, 63–5, 67, 75, 94
co-intentionally 22, 50
co-responsibility 13–15, 22, 80, 89–99, 104–6
cockpit effect 35–6
collaboration 50, 56, 59–62
communication *passim*; community 2, 48, 50–3, 71–6, 89–97, 113–14; competence 23, 27, 45–6, 61, 94;

cooperation 21–7, 32, 37, 45–6, 49, 56, 58–67, 70–3, 94; relation 20, 22–4, 48–9, 52, 61–2, 66–7, 74
communicative *a priori* 41–54, 56, 60, 69, 70, 100
consensus 48, 50, 61, 70, 73–4, 76, 91, 94; definitive 48, 53, 72, 108; practical 92; rational 92
cooperation 58, 61, 66, 90–2, 94, 104
Craig, R. T. 43, 113, 117
Crawford, M. 29, 117
criticism 97, 99–100, 105–11
Crookschank, F.G. 120
Cruz, A. M. 117

deindividuation 35
Davis, D. K. 115
Danescu-Niculescu-Mizil, C. 116
definitive justification 44, 70, 96–7, 103
DeFour, D. 117
DeFries, John C. 121
DeHaan, C. R. 121
DeNeve, K. 115
deontology 83, 95
Deuser, W. E. 115
Diener, E. 35, 117
discursive argumentation 47, 71–2
discursive attitude 53, 57
discursiveness 22, 48, 50, 53, 71, 83, 106–7
disinhibition 35
Dollard, J. 9, 17, 117
Doob, L. 17, 117
Dunbar, R. 58, 117

electronic cap of invisibility 35
Eliot, T. S. 26, 117
empathy 11, 35, 58; circuit 11; erosion of 11; genes 11
Erikson, E. 65, 117
ethics 93, 96–8, 102–4; of co-responsibility 89–98; discourse 93, 99, 104
Ezine, J.-L. 118

Farahidah, Y. Bt. M. 118
Ferguson, Ch. J. 31, 117
Ferguson, D. E. 117

Fidler, R. 19, 117
Fisk, N. 29, 117
Flax, R. 117
Foucault, M. 86, 109, 111–12, 115, 117–18
Frankl, V. E. 9–10, 118
freedom 28, 30, 49, 74, 81–2, 85, 92
Freud, S. 7, 10, 109, 118
Fritz, S. 117
Fromm, E. 8–10, 118
Fudge, M. 122
Fukuyama, F. 65, 118

Gadamer, H.-G. 2, 54, 61, 64, 94, 118
General Aggression Model 15
Gerald, E. 82, 118, 121
Giddens, A. 65, 118
Giumetti, G. W. 119
Gladwell, V. 121
Goban-Klas, T. 19, 118
Gouldner, A. 58, 62, 118
Grice, P. 58, 118

Habermas, J. 2, 22, 27, 48, 53, 55, 93, 95, 102–3, 108, 118
Hardin, R. 65, 118
Haron, H. 29, 118
Harry, D. 116
Harvey, A. 122
Heirman, W. 35, 118
Helenius, H. 122
Hill, K. 58, 118
Hmielowski, J. 117
Hobbes, T. 65, 118
Holba, A. M. 117
*homo communicativus* 2, 21, 45, 90
Horkheimer, M. 72, 112, 115
Hurtado, M. 118
Hutchens, M. 117
Hutchins, R. 80–2, 100

Ikonen, M. 122

Jagatic, T. 29, 119
Jakobson, R. 54, 119
Jakobsson, M. 119
Jędrzejewski, S. 119
Johnson, N. A. 119
Joinson, A. 35, 119

Jonas, H. 95, 116, 119
Jordan, T. 122

Kelly, J. 43, 119
Kettner, M. 115
knowledge 20, 22, 24, 26, 31, 42, 44–6, 48–9, 65, 69–71, 86–8, 91, 101, 104–9, 111–12; accompanying 46, 49, 65, 70; archeology of 106–7, 109, 112
Koskelainen, M. 122
Kowalski, R. M. 30, 35, 119
Krahé, B. 16, 119
Krumsiek, A. 30, 119
Krzysztofek, K. 29, 119
Kuhlmann, W. 44, 46–7, 53, 76, 90–2, 95–6, 119

Lattanner, M. R. 119
Lee, E.-J. 35, 119
Leskovec, J. 116
Levinson, P. 29–30, 37, 120
Levi-Strauss, C. 62, 120
Limber, S. P. 119
Lindroos, J. 122
linguistic communication practices 32, 44–7, 57
Locke, J. 65, 120
Lorenz, K. 7–8, 120
Luhmann, N. 65, 120
Luke, T. W. 122
Luntamo, T. 122
Lusk, R. 117

M*A*S (Media Accountability Systems) 83–4, 95
MacIver, A. 121
Malinowski, B. 56, 59, 62, 120
Mangion, C. 41, 120
Martens, E. 42, 120
mass communication 19, 52, 79, 86, 97
mass media 19–26, 28, 72–4, 84–5
mass neurotic triad 10
Mauss, M. 58, 62, 120
Mayer-Schönberger, V. 29, 35, 120
McClearn, G. E. 121
McCombs, M. 29, 120
McGuffin, P. 121

McQuail, D. 19, 30, 84, 100, 120
Mead, G. H. 64, 120
media communication 2, 18–19, 24–5, 27, 52, 84–5, 99; theories of 99, 100–1, 104–5
mediasphere 18–26
megamedia 19–26, 28–38, 74, 85, 86, 97, *passim*; communication 19–26, 73, 97, 99–100; space 56, 73, 75, 85–6, 99
Menczer, F. 119
Milgram, S. 14, 120
Miller, N. 17, 117
Miltner, K. 122
models of critique 105–7, 109, 111–12
Monroy-Hernández, A. 116
Mowrer, O. H. 17, 117
Murayama, K. 121
mutualism 60–2, 65, 75

naturalistic fallacy 101–2
Neisser, U. 66, 120
normativity 48, 85, 87, 99–104

Ogden, Ch. K. 120
Olweus, D. 35, 120

pain threshold 9, 11
Panovich, K. 116
Peterson, Th. 100, 121
philosophy of communication 41–2, 52; and communication philosophy 2, 37, 39–54, 59–60, 104
Pinker, S. 16, 30, 120–1
Plaisance, P.L. 84, 121
Plomin, R. 8, 121
Pokorna-Ignatowicz, K. 119
Pollack, D. 29, 121
Postmes, T. 35, 121
Prensky, M. 31, 121
presuppositions 46–7, 70–2, 74, 76, 96–7
principle of *do ut des* 62
proto-communication 61, 66
Przybylski, A. K. 29, 121
Putnam, R. 65, 121
Pyżalski, J. 30, 35–6, 38, 121

rationality 1, 47, 49–51, 57, 68–9, 71–6, 81–7, 95, 100, 106–114; discursive 66–8, 71–5, 87, 89, 96, 99, 104, 109
reciprocity 20, 23, 59, 62–3, 92; principle of 58, 62
responsibility 79–87, 89–90, 93, 95
Richards, I. A. 120
Ristkari, T. 122

Sahlins, M. 62, 121
Schnädelbach, H. 120
Schneier, B. 29, 121
Schramm, W. 100, 121
Schroeder, A. N. 119
self-matching 10
self-relevance 46, 104
self-relevant 46
Shultz, S. 117
Searle, J. 22, 41, 46, 53, 58, 64, 101–3, 121
Sears, R. 17, 117
Siebert, F. S. 72, 100, 121
Sierocka, B. 53, 56, 67, 100, 105, 122
Shaughnessy, K. 29, 122
Shepherd, T. 35, 122
Shoemaker, P. J. 29, 122
Simmel, G. 64, 122
Small, G. 29, 122
Smith, S. M. 117
social learning 9
Sourander, A. 35, 122
Sparks, C. 29, 122
Spears, R. 121
speech act 94, 101–3
Sperber, D. 63, 122
Srauy, S. 122
strict reflection 53, 70, 76, 90, 96, 98, 105

Suler, J. 30, 35, 122
Sztompka, P. 65, 67, 122

theory of frustration—aggression 9
Tomasello, M. 2, 22, 27, 58–61, 63–7, 122–3
Toulouse, C. 30, 122
transcendental pragmatics (TP) 43, 44–9, 69–72, 89–98, *passims*
transformation of Kantian's transcendentalism 44–5, 69
trust 23, 65–7, 75, 82–3, 85
Tulloch, J. 122

"unsinkability" of the content 35
Urbaniak, P. 84, 87, 122
Uslaner, E. 65, 123

Van Dijk, J. 29–30, 37, 123
Vargas, G. 116
Vorgan, G. 122
Vos, T. P. 122

Walrave, M. 118
Warneken, F. 60, 123
WikiLeaks 85–8
Willard, N. 38, 123
Wilson, D. 63, 122
Wilson, E. O. 7, 123
Wilson, K. 120
Wittgenstein, L. 6, 13, 27, 45, 47, 59–60, 64–5, 67, 101, 108, 123

Ybarra, G. J. 123
Young, K. 29, 123

Zimbardo, P. G. 14, 123
Zimmerman, A. G. 35, 123